SONSHINE

Also by Beverly ND Clopton

Surviving Pitfalls on the Path
A 40 Day Devotional

Heaven or Bust
Journey to Glory

Sonshine
Reflections of Faith

A Potpourri of Devotionals

Beverly ND Clopton

WordCrafts

Sonshine

Copyright © 2017 Beverly ND Clopton

ISBN: 978-1-948679-78-7

Cover design by Jonathan Grisham for Grisham Designs

All rights reserved. No part of this book may be reproduced, stored in any retrieval system, or transmitted in any form or by any means—electronic, mechanical, photocopy, recording, or otherwise—without the prior written permission of the publisher. The only exception is brief quotations for review purposes.

All Scripture quotations are taken from THE HOLY BIBLE, NEW INTERNATIONAL VERSION®, NIV® Copyright © 1973, 1978, 1984, 2011 by Biblica, Inc.™ Used by permission. All rights reserved worldwide.

Published by WordCrafts Press
Cody, Wyoming 82414
www.wordcrafts.net

I dedicate this book to my only son,
Quentin Christopher Clopton.
God's Gift
My joy. My heart.
My sonshine.

November 10, 2016
Mom

Contents

Introduction 1

Part One 3

Who Knew? 4
The Intersection of Dream Street and His Road Plan 7
Cross Wearer or Cross Bearer 10
The Cradle/The Cross 13
You Play the Hand You're Dealt 16
Stretch Out Your Hand 19
Whom Shall I Send? 22
Paradigm Shift 25
Hiding Under the Bedcover 28
No Worry Lines Here! 31
Embracing the Wait Time 34
Calling All Haters 37
The Fight of All Times: Common Sense Vs Faith 40
Where is Your Treasure? 44
Do You Believe in Miracles? 47
Filling Station 50
Come to Jesus Moment 53
Full-Time Followers 57
Of Donkeys & Fish & Text Messages 60
Are You Serious? 63

Part Two 67

Faith: Profession/Possession? 68
Practice Makes the Difference 70
Heard From the Lord Today? 72

Topsy-Turvy 75
Substituting 101 77
He Feels Your Pain 79
Automatic Praise 81
Ethical Infants 83
The Least Likely Source 85
Living Like Jesus 87
Frightening Words! 89
Sanctuary 91
Duality of Faith 93
Masked Christianity 95
Powerful Weakness 98
Headed Where? 101
Jesus Rest 104
What Do You Want Me To Give You? 107
Packing Pastors 109
Prodigal Son 112
Jehovah Jireh 115
Testing Time Testimony 118
Letting Go 121
Effective Prayer 124
Nothing is Impossible for God 127
Parallels 130
Who Writes the Music? 133
First Response Syndrome 136
Throwback Thursday 139
Outside the Box 142

Part Three 145

In—Not Of 146
Seasons 148
Never Say Goodbye 150
Sage Dust 152
What? How? Why 154

Who Is My Neighbor? 156
Tomorrow 158
Internal Cell Phone 160
21st Century Persecution 162
Ageless Provision 164
No Shame 166
Pray First 168
Little Billy Wisdom 170
21st Century Hospitality 172
The Human Condition 174
The Christian Shuffle 176
Peacemaker or Peacekeeper: Which Are You? 178
Resistant Surrender 180
Reluctant Servant 182
Worry Anonymous 184
Perversity 186
The Law—The Atonement 188
Two Roads 190
Fiery Furnaces 192
Soul Man 194
Fixer Syndrome 196
Even Marthas Finally Get It 198

PART FOUR 201

One Minute Reflections 201

Introduction

"Let this be written for a future generation, that a people not yet created may praise the Lord."

Psalm 102:18

I published my first book, *Heaven or Bust: Journey to Glory* in 2009. It is a compilation of 100 devotionals that include scripture and questions for reflection drawn from over two decades of my journaling. Writing in one form or another has been and is my calling card, and what I had believed I was destined to do until the day my mother, several weeks following my graduation from college said, "Bev, you have to get a real job that pays money. Writing is not a real job."

My dream of becoming a writer took a backseat to the reality of my life, and for nearly four decades I channeled my energy into teaching English language arts, composition and literature at the secondary school level; eventually moving into educational administration and management. For a time during those years, I wrote biographical short stories and periodically submitted articles to magazines and newspapers. As the "thank you, but no thank you" responses grew, I sought writer's refuge in journaling.

Following retirement and relocation in 2005, the dream deferred resurfaced; I repurposed my journal writing into the aforementioned book. Family and friends lauded my efforts and urged me to write another. When strangers joined their call for the next one,

I finally set about writing this book. It has taken a while. For too many years, interest and effort "waxed and waned." About two years ago, the pent-up emotions of wasting a gift I believe God gave me grabbed hold and wouldn't let go. The results: *Sonshine: Reflections of Faith. A Potpourri of Devotionals.*

I think of it as I do a large box of assorted chocolates. Sizes, shapes and flavors are varied and I select a piece or two to suit the mood of the moment. Likewise with this devotional, readers will make selections to satisfy their spiritual needs at different times: "soft center" times when life seems to be smooth sailing; "milk chocolate" times when a little warm encouragement hits the spot; "dark chocolate" times when challenges are overwhelming and all light is dimmed; "crunchy, nutty" times when a wakeup call is needed to get back into sync with the Lord's purposes. Whether inspired by scripture, other Christian writing, societal challenges or my own faith journey experiences, the devotionals speak to the yearnings of believers to connect to the source of our being–our Lord and Savior.

Following the unexpected hemorrhagic stroke my son suffered in January, 2016 and from which he is still recovering, I have added devotionals that speak directly to this season of my life and another new normal to which I have had to adjust.

I write to encourage today's believers and for those who in future years will seek inspiration to stay the course on this our journey to eternity.

Part One

1

Who Knew?

> *"For I know the plans I have for you,"* declares the Lord, *"plans to prosper you and not to harm you, plans to give you hope and a future..."*
>
> Jeremiah 29:11

Imagine the scene. The Israelites along with the surviving elders are conquered. Driven from Jerusalem in captivity, those who survived the holocaust live in exile in Babylon. A letter arrives from Jeremiah, with a word he proclaims is from the Lord Almighty. You can almost hear the sighs and groans as the elders open the text, expecting more bad news from this prophet of doom and gloom. Their sighs turn to murmurs of surprise and disbelief and probably raised eyebrows as they read. Plans to prosper us, to not bring us to harm, to give us a future? How can that be? We are exiles driven from our homeland, living as aliens among a foreign people. Where was this concern for us back when we were being run over, our homes and temple destroyed? What were your plans then when we were being harmed, when we had lost all hope for a future? Understandable questions when all you can see with the natural eye are pain and betrayal and devastation and defeat. I've been there. A loved one chooses to walk away from the marriage commitment. The plans and dreams you've shared gone in what seem a blink of the eye. Plunged into relationship exile, you wondered how this could be happening to you.

Who Knew?

I entitled this piece, "Who Knew?" because I've come to understand that though we think we know where our life story will lead us, we don't. We think we know because most of us prepare for the journey. We follow the plan, checking off the "To Dos" as we progress from dependence to a measure of independence, from toddling steps to firm gait, from ignorance to a measure of knowledge, from novice to veteran. And when the unexpected hits and devastates, we can't grasp that though we didn't know and most certainly can't discern a redeeming purpose from the circumstance that sends us into exile, God knows. That is the key to coming to terms with the faith we profess and struggle to live. God knows. Period. Not only does He know, he has a plan and has had a plan since He allowed our conception. His word to Jeremiah is true for each of us: "Before I formed you in the womb, I knew you..." (Jeremiah 1:5). He knows us. He knows the beginning and the end.

He knew the Jewish infant set adrift along the river banks, rescued and adopted by the Pharaoh's daughter would be named Moses. He knew that in adulthood, Moses would kill a man and be forced to flee his country and people to live in exile. He knew one day while in exile, Moses would move to the strange sight of a bush that "does not burn up" (Exodus 3:3). And with this step toward the unknown, Moses would live to become one of God's great servant leaders—the prophet of miracles whom the Bible says knew the Lord face to face. Who among them knew? God knew.

Most of us who have lived a reasonable number of years can probably look back and say of a circumstance or life event— "Who Knew?" Who knew what the outcome of an unexpected call from my seriously ill single-parent sister in Los Angeles on a Friday morning to tell me that she was having kidney surgery Monday would be? She didn't ask me to come, but when I said, "Who's going to take care of Gia?" (her one-year old daughter) and she replied, "I don't know. Stene is keeping her over the weekend. Momma can't come right now." I didn't have to think. I was on my way. Thankfully my principal was both sympathetic and supportive; he arranged for a substitute teacher and sent me off with his blessings. That unexpected "trip of mercy" as I called it placed me exactly where I'm convinced God planned for me to be, sort of like Moses in his papyrus basket at just the right spot for his life to dramatically change. It was during week two as I continued to wait for my mom to get to LA when a friend suggested I take a break, allow her daughter to babysit little Gia and attend a bridge party event. I hesitated. I was still wallowing in my relationship exile and really not up for celebratory gatherings. She was a caring friend and wouldn't take "No" for an answer. Reluctantly, I agreed and went.

Long story short: At that party unbeknown to me was my soulmate, the man who would in five years become my husband and to whom I would be married for 30 plus years before the Lord called him home. How could I know this trip was part of God's plan to prosper me, to give me hope and a future? Just like Moses had no way of nothing what his investigation of the burning bush would lead to, I had no idea what saying "Yes" to a party invite would ultimately bring. In both instances the Lord knew. From biblical accounts we know that the people who crossed the sea over dry land were glad God knew the plans he had for them and Moses. Those plans saved their lives. I too am glad that during that dark season of betrayal and loss, God's plans for me were in motion. My sister's illness brought me from across country into the unknown. Like Moses, I didn't hesitate. I simply went. And the joy of that decision and what God has allowed because of it sustain me still.

For Moses, the infant abandoned in the river and for me, abandoned by the person to whom I had shared the marriage bond, God's plans were in motion. Did we know? No. Who knew? God knew.

2

The Intersection of Dream Street and His Road Plan

"For I know the plans I have for you…"
Jeremiah 29:11

Continuing this discourse on God's plans for us in light of our experiences, I recall the poem "Dream Deferred" by writer Langston Hughes. It begins "What happens to a dream deferred?" After offering several possibilities in answer to the question, the poet concludes with these words: "Maybe it just sags like a heavy load. Or does it explode?" The word dream to which I refer is not the images we have during sleep. I use the word to reference the long-held ideas or goals toward which we aspire: our dreams or plans we make to achieve the desires of our hearts. I believe that when we meet God at the intersection of Dream Street and His Plan Road, that rendezvous spot across the street from Do It Your Way Café, our dreams and God's plans for us merge.

Let me pose the question: Are dreams unspoken prayers? Perhaps. I believe they can walk hand in hand if the dreams mirror God's plans and will bring glory to him. Consider the rather familiar story of Samuel's mother, Hannah, the barren wife of Elkanah. For years Hannah prayed (dreamed; had as her one and only goal) for a son. Her husband's second wife not only was busy being fruitful and multiplying, but in her spare time harassing Hannah for her inability to add to the family numbers. You can imagine the tension in the tent. What I like about Hannah is her persistence and her trust that if she keeps praying, God will bring her dream to fruition. She's at the desperation stage when one year at the temple she makes a vow to the Lord, saying "O, Lord Almighty, if you will only look upon your servant's misery and remember me, and not forget your servant but give her a son, then I will give him to the Lord for all the days of his life…" (I Samuel 1:11) In due time, the scriptures tell us, the Lord remembered Hannah. She conceived and bore a son whom she named Samuel, saying "Because I asked the Lord for him."

This story illustrates my premise that if we keep that appointment with God at that intersection of Dream Street and His Plan Road, He will hear and answer when our dreams manifest His plans for us. Hannah's dream came true. She had her son whom she nursed and nurtured until he was of age for her to keep her vow. She gave her son to the Lord's service in the temple under the tutelage of Eli, the priest. Samuel as we know went on to great servant leadership as priest and was used by God to anoint Israel's first king, Saul; and later to anoint David the future king of Israel. God's plan for Samuel and Hannah's dream met on the corner of Dream Street and His Plan Road. And just in case you're a little concerned that Hannah had to give up her son after all those years of praying and dreaming, don't be. Hannah and Elkanah added three more sons and two daughters to the family tree. Talk about answered prayer. Even when there's some bitterness mixed with the sweet, God's plan is the best concoction.

For years, Hannah's dream seemed to "sag like a heavy load." But one day in God's time that dream exploded, ignited by her unceasing fervent prayers, into the birth of the son for whom she dreamed. It's a reminder to us that unanswered prayers may weigh heavily upon us for an indeterminate time. That doesn't mean we should give up praying or dreaming.

If we stay focused on the dream—the prayer, God will respond.

The Intersection of Dream Street and His Road Plan

And I might add that often times even when we haven't been unceasing in our praying, God still moves on our behalf to bring his plan forward. We can all testify to difficult circumstances that have kept us awake at night—the lost job, the surprise doctor's report, the broken relationship, situations with the power to not just defer the dream, but to destroy it. But because we have an advocate in Jesus who intercedes on our behalf before the Father, our circumstances become our testimony of the goodness and faithfulness of God.

3

Cross Wearer or Cross Bearer

"...and anyone who does not take his cross and follow me is not worthy of me."

Matthew 10:38

"And anyone who does not carry his cross and follow me cannot be my disciple."

Luke 14:27

Can't you just imagine Jesus fighting the urge to send a "SMH" text message on His heavenly smartphone every time someone spies a cross in a jewelry display and gushes, "OMG! That's so beautiful. I'll take it. I love crosses." And why wouldn't He shake His heavenly head at the meaning the cross has come to symbolize—a striking piece of jewelry, often made of exquisite gems, fashioned as a necklace or bracelet or earring or pendant or a creative piece of art designed for accessorizing a home. I acknowledge that some people do buy and wear crosses as a symbol of their Christian faith. But many others have no such affiliation. For them the cross worn as a piece of jewelry is no different than an elephant earring or a butterfly bracelet. I also imagine that Christ is especially saddened by we who claim him Lord and Savior, who wear the symbol of salvation and yet display none of the attributes of discipleship.

In his book, *My Utmost for His Highest*, Oswald Chambers poses the question, "Is God getting His way with me, and are other people beginning to see God in my life more and more?" It's a fundamental question for all who have thrown in their lot with Christ. The cost of being a disciple requires more than a wave of the hand, a sway of the body to the rhythm of soul stirring music, the solemn recitation of creeds and dogmas or the wearing of a cross. The cost of being a disciple requires cross bearing. It is cross bearing that reveals your answer to Chamber's question. Only a will surrendered to Jesus can bear the weight of the cross. Just ask Simon of Cyrene. But carrying the cross today is much more complex than when Simon shouldered Jesus' wooden crossbeams. Today's cross is a cross of self-denial, sacrifice, obedience, service in kingdom building, and putting God first in everything. And it is with these crosses that we contemporary Christians stumble. Ours is a self-absorbed, consumeristic, image conscious generation, more concerned with the acquisition of goods and services that define our "success" than we are with cross carrying.

Yes, in our own time, we can point to people we identify as cross bearers: individuals who surrender their will to God's and in whom we see godly characteristics. In the larger community they are the missionaries and homeless shelter workers; they carry or bear the cross through their service in other countries and in disadvantaged communities here at home. They are joined by many others; some of whom are like my sister friend Donna who grows her striking head of hair until it reaches almost waist length and then has it cut to donate to the program that uses human hair to make wigs for cancer patients.

Yet even as we acknowledge these examples, we know they in no way balance the ledger. And as professed believers, we know clearly why we struggle with Jesus' call to take up our cross and follow Him. Face it. Cross-bearing has never and probably will never make the list of "Things to Do before You Die." It's just so hard, so inconvenient, so time consuming, so "not me", so old school, well just so "churchy." The time is long past when we can just claim Christ with our mouth, but not follow with our actions what His word says that looks like. And often our guilt-ridden solution (because I really am a Christian) is: another cross necklace with the cutest matching earrings, a one of a kind cross displayed proudly on the shelf in my living room, and one in my office if I can get away with it. Do I have enough of them to make me a crossbearer? No, I don't think so. One only gets to be a cross-carrier by heeding Jesus' word to surrender and follow Him, cross shouldered, allowing His Light to shine in all you do. To paraphrase the bard, all else is but a symbol worn by the unknowing and the knowing, full of flash and dash, signifying nothing.

4

The Cradle/The Cross

Today in the town of David a Savior has been born to you; he is Christ the Lord. This will be a sign to you: you will find a baby wrapped in cloths and lying in a manger.
                                                            Luke 2:11–12

For God was pleased to have all his fullness dwell in him, and through him to reconcile to himself all things, whether things on earth or things in heaven, by making peace through his blood, shed on the cross.
                                                            Colossians 1:19

In the previous devotional, I dealt with the cross, the object upon which Jesus gave his life for our sins to reconcile us with God the Father; and specifically, what Jesus says the cross was to mean for his followers and how that meaning has been compromised or corrupted over these many millenniums. Basically, the piece was an indictment of those who say they are believers, but do more wearing of the cross than they do of carrying it. In this piece, I want to delve a little more into the cross and its powerful significance for Christian believers. The scripture from the Gospel of Luke reminds us of Jesus's birth. He was born, wrapped in swaddling clothes and laid in a manger, a cradle as we would call it today. The Colossians passage gives insight into God's reasoning for both Jesus' birth and His eventual death on a cross. Both cradle and cross tell the story of God's salvation plan.

SonShine: Reflections of Faith

I volunteer in a non-profit hospital gift shop. All the proceeds from the sales go to the hospital to supplement the needs of the patients and staff. It happened to be the time of year that the gift shop decorators were "decking the halls" in preparation for the approaching holiday season. I was surprised when they began placing brown woven crosses tied at the crossbeam with a traditional plaid tartan holiday ribbon on the shelves. In fact, I actually muttered, "Why do we have these crosses on display as Christmas decorations? The cross has nothing to do with Christmas; it represents the Easter season and Jesus' crucifixion." A few days later, a sentence in one of my morning devotionals read, "The cradle without the cross misses the true meaning of Christ's birth." How could I have so missed the point?

Consider the impact babies have on us. I don't know many folks who don't like them. Their very innocence and dependence capture our hearts. Even the gruffest of us melt when we gaze into their eyes. And don't let them smile! We go absolutely gaga. And yet that is exactly what God sent us. A tiny baby! He wasn't a super hero or an avenging warrior, but a baby they called Jesus. His arrival and the story surrounding it inform the first of the great Christian holidays—Christmas. As believers we embrace baby Jesus at this time of the year more than any other. And people who don't even believe that Jesus is the son of God, born to the Virgin Mary as we do, still celebrate this traditional Christian tradition. Christian and non-Christian alike decorate homes and churches with representations of Mary, Joseph, shepherds, wise men, stable animals and of course baby Jesus in the manger. For believers these vignettes serve to remind us that Jesus was God's gift. At this time of year, we give no thought to His eventual death on the cross. Who's thinking about death at Christmas time? No one.

Oh, but I can imagine that every year at Christmas time, God is hoping that somebody will get the connection, that the baby is destined for death; and not just the ordinary death of all mortals. But a death preordained so that sinners would be saved. Beyond the sentimental, the impact upon mankind of baby Jesus lying in the cradle is not realized until 33 years later when He is hanging on the cross. God had a plan for salvation, but we forget that when we separate the birth from the death. He birthed Jesus to die so that we might be reconciled to the Creator and live. Without the cross, we would be separated still. The cradle and the cross must stand side by side, holy and divine links in the chain of God's salvation plan for His creation. The cross ties the bow around the cradle that held God's gift—Jesus Christ, the one whom we follow.

Now you know how this ends, right? During my very next volunteer shift, I bought myself a Christmas cross, complete with plaid red bow. Now with its prominence above my manger scene, ours is a testament of the "true meaning of Christ's birth," and what it means to follow the one who bore the cross for us.

5

You Play the Hand You're Dealt

And we know that in all things God works for the good of those who love him, who have been called according to his purpose.
                                                                Romans 8:28

Now Job wasn't around when Paul penned those words to the church at Rome. In fact, scripture doesn't suggest that he might have ever had such thoughts. But because we know Job's story, we wonder if those words inspired by God and written by Paul centuries later apply to him, to others who have faced difficult circumstances. Do the hardship stories of Job and others contradict or confirm that infinite God works for the good of those who love him and are called according to his purpose? And if you are Job or someone like Job, what do you do with the "hand you're dealt" that by all appearances is a losing one? The story of what Job did when dealt that devastating hand of loss of family and property and possessions is well known. Though he couldn't figure out what had caused such calamity, and despite the advice of his wife, he refused to curse God. In fact his philosophy was simple: *"Naked I came from my mother's womb, and naked I will depart. The Lord gave and the Lord has taken away; may the name of the Lord be praised."* (Job 1:21) And though Job's story starts on a decidedly negative note, the ending does indeed illustrate that God works for the good of folk who demonstrate their love for him, and for whom he has a purpose. Here we are thousands of years later and the story of Job is the one we turn to for encouragement when life throws a fast ball that literally knocks us off our feet—unexpected death of a loved one, loss of employment and subsequent loss of shelter and transportation, life threatening medical reports, natural disasters, man-made disasters, war and its attendant results. The list could go on. In each of these challenges, Job shows us how to play the hand we're dealt. Like Job we may question God, may even get angry at Him. We listen to what friends have to say about our situation. But in the end, after the dust settles, we realize that God is greater than we are; He is certainly more knowledgeable; He is responsible for our birth; He provides for our needs and wants and all we have and are come from Him. And despite what it may look like from a human perspective, He is working for our good.

And who can forget the story of Daniel and his three friends, God loving young men carried off as captives of war following the destruction of Jerusalem by King Nebuchadnezzar. Imagine the shock of having the privileged lifestyle snatched away. Living no longer as royalty being served, but as servants doing the serving! And to make matters even more difficult, the conqueror worships pagan gods. How do you play that hand? Consider the responses of Daniel and his friends. They did not forsake God. They did not curse their circumstances. They held onto their faith as they prayed for God's guidance and protection. Even the king's issuance of the death penalty via a fiery furnace and a den of lions for their refusal to bow to idols did not alter their resolve to serve the one and only living God. That's how they played the hand they were dealt, trusting God and believing that He was working for their good.

I'm going to get really personal now. I too know what it means to play the hand you're dealt. Nothing had prepared me for my husband's unexpected sudden death. Oh, I knew we were getting older, but I figured we had at least another 20–30 years together before the Lord called one of us home. Even when he said he knew he was going first, I brushed off his comments as idle talk. In retrospect, I figure he knew something I didn't. But anyway, when the cards were dealt that Sunday evening, I was caught like the proverbial deer in headlights. I couldn't believe the "car" speeding toward me would hit and take me in a moment to the "valley of shadow and death." But there I was, widowed in a new place without the support system I would have had in the place we lived before relocating. Did I question God's timing? Yes. Did I cry in anguish, "Why, Lord, Why?" Yes. Did I wallow sometime in self-pity? Yes. But I truly believe I was saved by following my brother's suggestion to me on the day of Earl's interment—"Read the book of Job, one chapter a day." That daily reading coupled with the devotionals in a book my daughter in law gave me helped me fashion a new normal. I picked up the cards representing my "what now" and began to play this hand life had dealt. I was able to do that not only by staying in God's word, but more importantly by trusting that His word is true. As I stayed in God's presence through prayer, meditation and journaling, I grew stronger. Indeed, Paul's words in I Corinthians 1:4 proved more than true: *"Praise be to the God and Father of our Lord Jesus Christ, the Father of compassion and the God of all comfort, who comforts us in all our troubles, so that we can comfort those in any trouble with the comfort we ourselves have received from God."* That scripture describes exactly what has been my experience as I have offered comfort to women who face the same tragedy. As I reflect upon these past eleven years, I can see how even in this, God was working for my good. Like Job, I can declare, *"Shall we accept good from God, and not trouble?"* The answer of course is "No." We trust Him when His blessings bombard us and we trust Him when the unthinkable unhinges us. Whatever the hand we're dealt, we play it in absolute trust that He is working for our good. And we follow Him because he's the master player no matter how the cards fall.

6

Stretch Out Your Hand

Going on from that place, he went into their synagogue, and a man with a shriveled hand was there... The he said to the man, "Stretch out your hand." So he stretched it out and it was completely restored, just as sound as the other.

Matthew 12:9, 13

Most Christians are familiar with this miracle story in the Gospel of Matthew. In it Jesus refutes the Pharisees, the "haters" of his day, who wanted to trap him into admission that his actions were against the law. "Is it lawful to heal on the Sabbath?" they asked Him. At that point, Jesus turned to the man with the shriveled man and the exchange recorded above occurred. Jesus seized a teachable moment and declared it is indeed lawful to do "good" on the Sabbath. Aside from putting the Pharisees in their place, Jesus in this interaction with a disabled man teaches an even greater lesson, one especially relevant today.

Though we may not suffer physical disabilities like this man did, we all have something about us that needs restoration or healing. Maybe your attitude is easily bent out of shape. The chip you carry on your shoulder like an epaulet on a uniform keeps most folk at a distance. If the grocery store line is held up by a mother with kids in tow because she doesn't have quite enough to pay the bill and is sheepishly putting some things back, you bristle and mutter, "Good grief. Why did you put all that stuff in the basket in the first place? You know you didn't have enough money (food stamps)!" The thought of "paying forward" never crosses your mind because at that moment, your attitude is "shriveled." It doesn't take much to set off the person whose attitude needs major adjustment.

Our spirits too can suffer from the affliction of being "shriveled." Let something go wrong or not in our favor and we are renown for the pity parties we throw. Our spirits rise and fall with the happenings of our lives; and a downward happening sends us into a downward spin. We suffer from what I call "shriveled spirit syndrome." And let's be honest. Sometimes it's our deformed behavior that shouts the need for reformation. We gossip; we speak ill-considered words; we are intolerant; we practice favoritism; we cheat; we invest more time and money in our own pleasures than we do in nurturing our children or supporting our elderly. The list is endless. We even sit inside the temple, in the seat on our pew that everyone knows not to sit in, with arms folded, daring the Holy Spirit to approach us. Our "shriveled behaviors" block the transformation God is so eager and willing to give. Like the man who did not speak to Jesus as he passed, we remain silent. We seem bent on handling our issues with no help from the Master Healer, Restorer and Problem Solver.

The good news is that Jesus is no different today than He was that day outside the temple with the man whose hand was shriveled. He wants to make a point. He wants us to say, "Heal me; fix me." But even when we are like the man in the story and don't ask Jesus for help, He does it anyway.

Today his command, "Stretch out your hand" is directed to us in countless ways. Perhaps what you need to stretch out to Him is your crippled financial situation. Or maybe your witness as a disciple has withered and it needs to be stretched toward the Savior. Your shriveled hand could be your busy schedule that hinders your prayer or Bible study time. Whatever your shriveled condition, Jesus wants you do what the man outside the temple did. He did not hesitate or question; he obeyed the Lord's command and stretched his hand. That act of faith on his part was rewarded. We can only speculate what the outcome might have been had he done otherwise. Would Jesus have still healed his deformity? We don't know. What we do know is Jesus stands ready in our situations to heal, to restore and to make whole, not just our physical inadequacies, but our spiritual ones as well. To live in God's promises, we must do something. Our faith and our actions must operate in concert. We are not called to passivity. We are justified both by what we do (stretching our "hand") and our absolute faith in God's response.

7

Whom Shall I Send?

I heard the voice of the Lord saying, "Whom shall I send? And who will go for us?"

Isaiah 6:8

Imagine the prophet Isaiah at that moment when he heard God ask these two questions. Juxtapose this picture of Isaiah about to answer with the scene at the Sea of Galilee as Jesus walks by and calls out to two fishermen, "Come. Follow me." Can you see yourself responding as they did? Isaiah, eagerly answering, "Here I am. Send me." The disciples, dropping their nets and leaving their very livelihood to fall in step behind the Christ? I don't know about you, but I probably would have had to think a moment, a long moment at that. And if the truth is told what I and most folk I know would do is call or text our BFFs to describe what just happened. And then try to figure out what it really means and what might happen if it doesn't work out and what am I supposed to do with all the stuff on my plate already.

But these two instances of immediate response to God's call suggest that what these individuals possessed is what all disciples of Jesus Christ need—a willing spirit, an openness and receptivity to a life lived in and for God. Note that they did not pause to think or debate about the invitation. There was no "Did I hear him right?" moment. When God speaks there is always clarity for He is a forthright God. In Isaiah's moment, God expressed a need for someone to serve. Isaiah stepped up to the plate, bat in hand, ready for the field in which he was to prophesy. Simon and John didn't hesitate; didn't try to figure the cost of a lost day's work. They simply followed. Wherever Jesus was going, they decided to go with Him. In both instances there was no recorded discussion about possible ramifications or consequences of obeying the call.

Perhaps the reason so many of us live resisting God's call to move out in faith wherever He wishes us to is because we misunderstand His purposes. I think our resistance comes from our natural bent toward self-determination and self-reliance. To hear and respond affirmatively to the Lord's call requires a surrendered spirit and willing posture. God is always seeking the willing spirit, those who surrender their desires to further His. And the reality is that once we confess Jesus as Lord and Savior and take on the mantle of Christianity, we can no longer be like those who hesitate, who first weigh the consequences of service, who must first collaborate regarding the feasibility of the call, who think we know it all. Yes, Isaiah was a prophet, but he was human. I speculate that even as he answered, "Here I am. Send me," he considered what going for God would mean. Would he have the skills to accomplish whatever it was God wanted. Those are reasonable thoughts. But as scripture tells us, Isaiah went forth in God's strength to proclaim the Lord's messages to the people as God so willed. The disciples too moved out in faith, but I can hear them whispering to each other, just out of Jesus' hearing, "Where do you think he's leading us? What will we have to do? Can we do what he wants? But as true believers we don't allow those thoughts or questions to define us. We are the resurrected Isaiah, Simon and Andrew and all the others in our biblical history who heard the call and followed.

In the midst of the world's lingering problems, God is still asking these same kinds of questions and Jesus is still calling, "Follow me." True, the lures of the secular tempt us more and more away from godliness and obedience. But as Christians we strive to leave the pursuit of anything that does not line up with the call to "Come and go for us." And we don't get hung up on the idea that to follow or go means only the mission field efforts. These are vital, but so are our efforts where God has placed us in our home, our school, our church, our community, our place of work, our place of leisure. The call to go for God, to follow Christ is ubiquitous. Whenever you extend yourself in service or support, when you go the extra mile to uplift someone else, when you don't weigh the cost of assisting those in need, when you speak out and up for the downtrodden, when it's no longer about you, but about the God you claim as Savior, then you are answering the call. You are following.

8

Paradigm Shift

"...Do not be afraid, Mary, you have found favor with God."
Luke 1:30

"Saul, Saul, why do you persecute me?"
Acts 26:14

Going about their normal routines, both teenage Mary and young adult Paul had little inkling that God was about to turn their lives upside down and create a radical shift in their perceptions of who they were and who God was. An imminent paradigm shift was underway, one that would change the thinking of humankind forever. We know both their stories. Mary, not married but engaged to Joseph, is told by an angel that she will in her virginal state give birth to God's son. She was a simple small-town girl with no attributes recorded in scripture that would explain why the angel of the Lord came to her with this announcement. We can imagine that she was an obedient teenager, modest and yes, excited about her impending wedding. We can hear the giggles as she and her friends chatter and plan for the big day! And then one morning (though the scripture doesn't give the time of day), the salutation: "Greetings, you who are highly favored! The Lord is with you," brings that seminal intrusion. And Saul, the fiery Jewish persecutor of the followers of the way, determined in his crusade to crush the Jesus movement sweeping the region. He was an ambitious young man making his mark on the world and certainly impressing the Jewish leaders with his fervor. He was what we today would call someone "on the fast track." As he brought back to Jerusalem those converts to Jesus, he could expect at some point to be rewarded: maybe an exalted position, certainly recognition as a mover and shaker in stamping out Christian heresy; nothing to be easily dismissed. But God intruded. On his way to Damascus with a commission (perhaps our equivalent of a search warrant) from the high priest to persecute the followers of Jesus, a voice speaks to him in Aramaic, the words quoted above from Acts 26:14. A seminal intrusion.

Because of these and other biblical examples of God's intrusive activity in human history, it should not surprise us today as Christian believers when God does the same in our lives. In fact, we should live in expectancy of just that. From the moment we accept Christ as our Lord and Savior, we should anticipate that our lives will never be the same, never quite what we had planned, perhaps never progress along the paths we envisioned. This should be our attitude as we seek each day to live in his will and purpose for us. Because we know from our biblical history how He works, we certainly should not be surprised when the unexpected occurs. We make it to the position in the company to which we've aspired and are favorably compensated for our hard work. Without warning, a notice comes announcing that due to escalating losses and outsourcing, our position will be phased out.

Or the youngest child finally heads off to college. The long-awaited empty nest season arrives and with glee you line up your plans for the things you've put on the back burner while raising your family. And before you can complete the form to begin your watercolor painting class or try your first yoga position glammed in your yoga outfit, the phone rings. It's your oldest child, the mother of your three grandchildren. Between the tears and gulps for air, you piece together that the marriage is on the rocks. She asks if she and they can come home to live with you. And the house is full again. Or even more devastating as was my experience. You sit watching something inane on television with your beloved spouse; and without warning, a blessed union of 30 plus years comes to an end as he succumbs to a fatal heart attack. God intrusions. And don't let me give the impression that these intrusions are always negative. They are not. God intrudes and shifts paradigms in positive ways also. Just ask the infertile couple who had given up on their dream of being parents, settled into a childless lifestyle and then discover that those "Wednesday's Children Full of Woe" are just waiting for people like them to become official moms and dads. Even the homeless man living on the street and in a shelter on winter nights experiences one of those God intrusions when he's finally offered a job that allows him to leave that cardboard box life forever.

As believers we live only one way – expecting God to surprise us, to intrude, to bring about His will for us, to change our way of thinking and living so that as His disciples, others see what it means to hear His call and to follow Him.

9

HIDING UNDER THE BEDCOVER

This is what the Lord says: "In the time of my favor, I will answer you, and in the day of salvation, I will help you…"
                                                           Isaiah 49:8

I'm an avid newspaper comics fan. Seldom does a morning pass without my daily dose of comics-induced laughter. One of my favorites is "Stone Soup." For several episodes now the widowed mom who has finally said "Yes" to a proposal of marriage finds herself cowering in fear and uncertainty because her soon to be husband was almost killed in a motorcycle accident. That he is on his way to a full recovery doesn't help mom's anxiety. She spends her time either hunched under her desk or more recently in bed with the covers drawn over her head. She's afraid a second marriage might end as did the first with this husband dying. Kind of serious stuff, but the humor evolves around her family, most especially her mom, as they attempt to pull her out of this doom and gloom outlook and insure she doesn't become a "runaway bride."

The story line reminds me of how easily we slip into similar dispositions when things aren't going the way we wish; when we fall under the mesmerizingly dismal view of the world as heralded by bold newspaper headlines. Other media add to our sense that the "world has gone to hell in a handbasket" with their reports of the nation's downward spiral economically, culturally and politically. Protests dot the landscape as communities react to the latest police killing of African American men. National achievement scores for select children in public schools continue below proficiency. Many people struggle still with unemployment or underemployment. And most upsetting of all in the world's largest Christian nation, the issue of race still defines this century. Some would say if ever there was a need for God's intervention and His grace it is now. But too often in times like these, even believers forget that His grace is poured forth all the time. Perhaps what we need to do is come from under the covers and claim the grace available to us no matter the circumstances. We turn to the words of encouragement offered in one of the Apostle Paul's letters to the church at Corinth. He tells us as he told them, "As God's fellow workers we urge you not to receive God's grace in vain." For he says, 'in the time of my favor I heard you and in the day of salvation I helped you.'" And Paul concludes with words that are as relevant today as they were then: "I tell you, now is the time of Gods' favor, now is the day of salvation."

Yes, as believers we do not have the privilege of hiding under the desk, the bedcovers, behind the wall of indifference or in a closet of hopelessness. Even if everyone else is surrendering to the dogmas of doom and gloom, we do not. That pathway negates the grace under which we live. God isn't asleep or on vacation. He knows about our current and future predicaments. I think what He's doing is watching to see how His followers respond. Are we like everyone else? Or do we understand that it is exactly when we have nothing upon which to depend except Him, that God is most available to us? That usually His time of favor is not during times of prosperity, but just the opposite?

Let's be real. When we are doing well, He doesn't hear from us too often; maybe the perfunctory prayer of thanks or an occasional "Thank you, Jesus," when prompted by the minister on Sunday morning. We're busy relishing the good times. The time of His favor has a way of revealing itself when prosperity fades or hits rock bottom—a time just like today. As believers we understand that if this is the time of His favor, it is also the day of His salvation. We take God's word as truth. When He says He will help us, we believe Him despite evidence to the contrary. We are called in following Him to live in ways that point to His sufficiency. Times such as these are fertile for living a Christ-like life, a life that continues to bear fruit for the kingdom. Jobless, without adequate health care, unfavorable report from the physician, foreclosed home, rent past due, dependent upon the food bank or local church for groceries. No matter. We do not despair as those who have no hope. We have His grace; it is sufficient for the day, for the time as we follow Him in faith.

10

No Worry Lines Here!

"Therefore I tell you, do not worry about your life… Who of you by worrying can add a single hour to his life? …Therefore do not worry about tomorrow, for tomorrow will worry about itself…"
Matthew 6:25, 27, 34

Interested in spending a little less money on facial creams touted to reduce, erase, and banish those horizontal lines that are trying to take up residence across your forehead? You know the ones I mean. The ones that suggest you might be a little older than you are. Yes, those lines, the ones skin specialists call "worry lines." Well, you are in luck today. I may have just the remedy, if not for the ones already in place, at least for those cousins of theirs making plans to join them. If you've been in church for even the least amount of time, you've probably heard the scriptural references above spoken and heard a choir sing, "I Know Who Holds Tomorrow," with its lyrics *"I don't worry over the future…"* Between the scriptures and the preaching and the singing, the message is clear. We are not to worry, especially if we are believers. And if I were a betting person, I'd wager you've thought and voiced on numerous occasions, "What a challenging command from the Savior these words are!" Jesus was speaking his Sermon on the Mount when he made those declarations and I imagine even the disciples were struggling with the "how" of obeying them; just as we do who read and hear them today.

SonShine: Reflections of Faith

Now perhaps the seasoned saints among us who are matured in their faith may find compliance with the command less difficult. If God has blessed you to see the sixth decade and beyond, life's experiences have probably taught that worrying is useless; energy expended without return. But for those yet to mark that season of life, this is a hard teaching. The struggle isn't because His words are vague. "Do not worry about your life" (or the lives of your loved ones, I add). Simple words. It is their implication that gives pause. When the economy is on the downturn and jobs are lost; when the unemployment stipend stops coming; when resume after resume goes unanswered; when there is little or no health insurance and the kids keep getting sick; when the bills are past due and the creditors call so often you no longer pick up the phone; when the car breaks down and there's no money to pay for repairs; when the rent is raised or the mortgage payment falls behind; when those you love demand more of you than you have to give; when the joy of living jades, how in God's name are you supposed to not worry?

I'm not naïve enough to suggest that these issues aren't peace disturbers and anxiety increasers. What I will suggest is that worrying won't drive them away; worrying will only deepen those frown lines and encourage their cousins to join them. And that's what we want to avoid. Take a moment to ponder the truth of these lyrics from the old hymn, "Is Your All on the Altar?" *Oh, we never can know what the Lord will bestow of the blessings for which we have prayed; till our body and soul He doth fully control and our all on the altar is laid.* In these words, I think we find recourse for how to live this teaching. When we are faithful in placing all our concerns and worry at the altar of Christ's sacrifice, we master the principle of worry-free living. In giving over to Jesus all that worries us, we learn to focus on Him and not our problems. In that surrendered posture, His peace steals over us. The problems don't typically vanish overnight, but what does vanish is our worrying about them. We find peace in our problems because we trust that God will answer our prayers. We don't know when or how, but we trust anyway. We learn to live one day at a time and offer thanksgiving for whatever the day brings. We discover it's impossible to worry and praise at the same time. And as we grow in this discipline of not worrying, we find greater peace in His presence; the place He wants us anyway. And the icing on the cake—as we follow His call to "not worry," we shut the door on those worry line cousins and send them packing!

11

Embracing the Wait Time

"...but those who wait on the Lord..."

Isaiah 40:31

In opening her sermon, the pastor read from the Book of Isaiah, chapter 40, and verses 28–31. *"Do you not know? Have you not heard? The Lord is the everlasting God, the Creator of the ends of the earth. He will not grow tired or weary, and his understanding no one can fathom. He gives strength to the weary and increases the power of the weak. Even youths grow tired and weary, and young men stumble and fall; but those who wait on the Lord will renew their strength. They will soar on wings like eagles; they will run and not grow weary; they will walk and not be faint."* And without further comment, she sat down. It was quite an awkward moment as it was evident there was more to the sermon than just the scripture, yet quietly she sat. Perhaps a couple of minutes passed before she returned to the lectern with the comment, "I wondered how many could wait with me." The next day remembering her reality check in this matter of learning to wait on the Lord, I pondered the prophet's words again. The condition for our realization of God's promise of being able to soar like eagles, to run without becoming fatigued and to walk without fainting is dependent upon our ability to wait for Him. When we read it, it seems a simple notion, but putting it into practice is more of a challenge, as I soon discovered. That morning during my devotional period I attempted to insert some "waiting on the Lord" time, an intentional period of silence in His presence before beginning my journaling. As had occurred during the morning worship service, it was a challenge to just wait. What ought to have been a "centering moment" was anything but. My mind was the culprit. Within minutes it began darting all over the place. If waiting on the Lord requires complete focus on Him and His will, my practice of this faith discipline is obviously still in the infant stages. Try as I might, I could not just sit quietly and wait on the Lord without my thoughts mushrooming into a cloud of major and minor sub thoughts that totally nullified my wait time. I suspect this was my experience because I am like many believers; I have a schedule to keep. Yes, I am faithful in my daily practice of reading Scripture, praying, contemplating the wisdom of several devotional resources and the words of renowned Christian writers and concluding with my own journaling of insights and revelations. Yet other than the five minutes I give to sipping my coffee, I haven't managed to truly "wait." And when I do sit a little longer in an effort to wait, my mind is not centered on the Lord's will. Rather it's off to the races with my stuff, my day's agenda, my never-ending "To Do List, my dreams and schemes, if you will.

The pastor made a point that Sunday. To realize God's promise inherent in these words of the prophet, we must muster the will to develop this "waiting" discipline. We forfeit all God has for us, His direction and guidance, His strength, His power when we don't wait for Him. Perhaps it was what Jesus had in mind when He asked Peter and the other disciples to, "Stay here and watch with me," as He prayed in the Garden of Gethsemane before His arrest. Could they wait for the Lord as He prayed? No, they could not. Jesus' words speak to us in our similar failure to wait. *"What! Could you not watch with me one hour?"* An hour, we say; we struggle to wait for Him five minutes without "falling asleep", our minds focused on things unrelated to a moment of stillness and prayer. And saddest of all, our failure to wait on the Lord blocks the blessings He desires to bestow. Imagine what might have happened in the garden and in the outer courtyard if Peter and company had waited/watched and prayed instead of sleeping: no ear severed, no disciples in fearful flight and no denials before the cock crowed three times. Instead of panic and fear, time spent waiting, watching and praying would have strengthened them for the ordeal ahead.

And what might it mean for us if we too could wait on the Lord? Maybe waiting would silence our tongue long enough in a heated argument to keep words being spoken that later we regret. Maybe waiting would send us to our knees in prayer when the doctor's report is unexpected or not what we wanted to hear rather than to the nearest bar to drown our fears in a bottle. Perhaps even waiting on God would keep us grounded in faith and filled with thanksgiving when the big promotion comes instead of glorying in how awesome we are in our fields of endeavor. In her demonstration of "waiting," the pastor was on point. We understand waiting is more than the physical aspect of being still though that has its value; more importantly, waiting on God is an intentional pursuit to seek His guidance and wisdom through prayer and to grow in discernment by staying in His word. Miraculous things happen when we wait on God. Read Isaiah 40:30–31 again to confirm it. Wait for Him and then follow where He leads. Really, it's a no-brainer!

12

CALLING ALL HATERS

But some of them said, "Could not he who opened the eyes of the blind man have kept this man from dying?" (John 11:37)

The dictionary defines *hater* as a person who greatly dislikes a specified person or thing. But since the late 1970s it's been used in popular culture as a term that describes someone who is motivated by envy, jealousy or maliciousness. As the one-word term evolved into the phrase, "haters gonna hate," its use has become an easy catchphrase within the social media generation to identify those who easily malign or find fault with others. And though the word may not have been used two thousand years ago, the attitude behind the word surely existed. Let's take a closer look at this passage from the Gospel of John. We'll see that in the crowds that followed Jesus were some serious "haters." While engaged in ministry in another town, Jesus receives word that a friend Lazarus is sick; in the message his sisters urge Jesus to come back to Bethany, in all probability hoping that Jesus would do for Lazarus what He has become known to do: heal and restore. Unfortunately, before Jesus gets there, Lazarus dies. Jesus arrives upon a scene filled with sorrowful mourners and weeping family members. One of the sisters even chastises Jesus with the comment, "Lord, if you had been here, my brother would not have died." Deeply troubled, Jesus too weeps as He is led to tomb where they have laid the body.

Are you getting this biblical picture? A brother, a friend, a member of the community has died and been buried for four days.

Grief, sorrow and pain reign. Even knowing what He was about to do, Jesus is overcome with emotion Himself and sheds tears. The Jews, according to the scripture, proclaim how much He must have loved Lazarus as measured by this reaction to his death. And rather than sympathize or offer words of comfort, listen to what some in the crowd are heard to mutter. *"Humph. If he's so powerful, couldn't he have saved Lazarus? I mean anybody who can make a blind man see could surely have prevented this death he's so torn up about."* (My paraphrase) In this bereavement moment, these "haters" did what haters do best; they found fault; they criticized. And because the proverbial apple doesn't fall far from the tree, haters today are no different than their biblical haters. No matter who we are or where we are or how we are, there are people who feel compelled to point out what we are not doing, should have done or need to do. Their skillset is fault-finding, often flavored with attitudes of envy or jealousy. *"Oh, she got that promotion because her daddy went to school with the CEO."* *"Well, who did you expect the coach to start as quarterback? His parents are big time contributors to the booster club."* *"Okay, so you lost the weight, but what are you going to do about those love handles?"* And as our scripture passage shows, sometimes our haters are those who we think are fellow followers of Jesus. Those snarly comments didn't come from the Romans, but from people who seemed to be friends of Lazarus and his family. Yet in the midst of this funereal gathering, they spoke words only a hater would speak: *"Couldn't he have done more?"*

It should come as no surprise that contemporary followers have similar experiences. Even in the faith community where we are surrounded by those we call sisters and brothers in Christ, people will manifest the "haters gonna hate" syndrome. *"Oh my, she's certainly not the person who needs to welcome the visitors. Her grammar is awful!"* *"Who decided he's the best choice to direct the choir? He just finished college. What does he know?"* *"As pastor, you'd think he'd know better than to do that."* So how do serious followers of Jesus respond when confronted by or witness haters in action? The Gospel records no responses to the haters, including none from Jesus or the disciples. It appears the commentary from the haters was ignored by all those at the scene. And it's easy to understand why. What they spoke was inconsequential as Jesus demonstrated His power over death itself by restoring Lazarus' life. And it is here I think we find the answer to the question. Rather than feed the haters with argument or reason, perhaps we simply ignore them. Jesus knew how that story would end; it was all done for God's glory. In post biblical times, we followers of Christ also know how the second half of the story will end. We need not be goaded by the haters; Jesus is as powerful today as He was then. The call to follow Him may sometimes mean not allowing ourselves to be distracted by the haters; they do what they do. We keep our eyes on Jesus. He knew what He was doing then; He knows what He's doing now. Unrepentant haters will receive their due.

13

The Fight of All Times:
Common Sense Vs Faith

Still another said, "I will follow you, Lord, but..."

Luke 9:61

Boxing fans will argue into the night if asked, "What's the greatest fight of all times?" Some old-timers will declare the 1938 Louis vs Schmeling battle the most important in ring history. Others will recall the Muhammad Ali era and his 1971 and 1974 bouts with Joe Frazier and George Foreman, respectively to be the greatest boxing contests of all times. Those who consider themselves boxing experts will swear there are no matches to rival the Tunney–Dempsey battle in 1927 or the Jack Johnson–James Jeffries throw down in 1910. Even I can recall the hype of the 1999 Felix Trinidad–Oscar De La Hoya match. But none of these or any other heralded pugilistic events can match the intensity and ferociousness of the fight that began over 2,000 years ago and continues to this moment: the battle between man's common sense and the faith required to take Jesus at His word.

In one corner, mentored by infamous coach, Devious Doubter is the long-time brawler, Common Sense. Considered by many the friend most needed to navigate life's journey, he is favored by the odd makers. And in the opposing corner, under the guidance of steadfast coach Firm Believer is Faith, thought to be the underdog in what the marquee bills: "The Fight of All Times."

The Fight of All Times: Common Sense Vs Faith

Oswald Chambers paints the perfect word picture of this fight between common sense and our faith in God when he writes, "Supposing God tells you to do something which is an enormous test to your common sense, what are you going to do…? Yes, but—supposing I do obey God in this matter, what about…? …Yes, I will obey God if He will let me use my common sense, but don't ask me to take a step in the dark… At the bar of common-sense Jesus Christ's statements may seem mad…" And herein is the rivalry that confronts the believer. Clothed in both common sense and faith, how do we not just hear the word, but actually do it, especially when it seems nonsensical.

The ringmaster beckons Common Sense and Faith to center ring; the bell sounds and round one is underway. "Follow me," Jesus says to a man who walks along with him. *"Lord, first let me go and bury my father,"* he man replies. *Jesus responds to him, "Let the dead bury their own dead, but you go and proclaim the kingdom of God." "Still another said, 'I will follow you, Lord; but first let me go back and say good-bye to my family.'" Jesus replies, "No one who puts his hand to the plow and looks back is fit for service in the kingdom of God."* (Luke 9:57–62) Common Sense throws the first punch—It's your responsibility to bury your parent; who else is supposed to do it? How can you not say farewell to your loved ones before you embark on a journey to God knows where? This is crazy talk. Do the right thing! Undaunted, Faith blocks – For the believer, proclaiming the kingdom and keeping your eye on the prize has far greater value. Attending to the call of Jesus far outweighs any earthly concerns. Jesus said, *"The harvest is plentiful, but the workers are few."* As believers our call is clear. Nothing takes precedence over the Lord's call on our lives. By faith we press onward confident that God will provide. The bell rings and the adversaries return to their respective corner.

As the second round gets underway, Common Sense dances to the center of the ring and lashes out – God says you are to do what? He tells you *"Do not worry about your life, what you will eat or drink, or about your body, what you will wear?"* (Matthew 6:25–33) Well, what about your children? Are they also to go without these necessities of life? Is this what Jesus is asking you to do? How can you not worry if these things are not in place for you and your family? That makes no sense! So caught up in his oratory, Common Sense doesn't see Faith's right hand, guided by the Father, as it hits its mark: Jesus says, *"Who of you by worrying can add anything to your life?...So do not worry, ...your heavenly Father knows that you need them...But seek first his kingdom and his righteousness and all these things will be given to you as well."* (Matthew 6:25–33) As believers we trust God's word that "faith is being sure of what we hope and certain of what we do not see." (Hebrews 11:1) And this is our certainty even in circumstances that appear otherwise – circumstances in which common sense says, "No way."

From all appearances, as the bell sounds to start the final round, the scorecards are close. All are hoping this will be the knockout round. Common Sense appears tired, battered even, the pep in his step gone. Faith takes the center ring and is clearly on the offensive. Yes, he begins. You led the jeering and laughter when Noah, after being warned of things not yet seen, began building that ark. And in doing so he *"became heir of the righteousness that comes by faith."*

That was you, Common Sense, who tried to persuade Abraham that it was foolish to heed God's call to go to a place he would receive as an inheritance even though he did not know where he was going. But by faith he went and made his home in the Promised Land. And later when God told Abraham to sacrifice the son through whom God's promises were to be realized, Abraham ignored you Common Sense, and in faith offered up Isaac as God so directed. And it was by faith and not their common sense that the people passed through the Red Sea as on dry land. (Hebrews 11:1–29) And was it not by faith rather than common sense that the woman with the issue of blood knew that if she could but touch the hem of Jesus' garment she would be healed. (Mark 5:25–29)

The Fight of All Times: Common Sense Vs Faith

Pandemonium breaks out as the crowd joins Faith's litany. Testimonies of faith getting them through difficult times when common sense told them it was not possible fill the arena. As the final bell rings, there is no doubt to which the victory belt belongs. Yes, it's risky and often scary to step out on faith when common sense says, "Yes, but what about…?" But the life of the believer is built on nothing less. Faith will carry you through the rounds; Faith will secure the victory every time.

14

WHERE IS YOUR TREASURE?

For where your treasure is, there your heart will be also.
                                                    Mathew 6:21
For all that is in the world—the desires of the flesh and the desires of the eyes and pride in possession—is not from the Father but is from the world.
                                                    1 John 2:16

Scripture cautions us against loving the world or the things in it. Why? It's impossible to love God and world; Satan is god of the world and there is no way we can give allegiance to both. Ultimately, we are forced to choose. And it's hard. We want what God offers: forgiveness, salvation, peace and eternal life but we also enjoy the secular enticements. They tempt us at every turn. Oh, that handbag is to die for! Look at those shoes, and they're on sale! Those earrings are perfect, just my style. Wow, can't you see us driving that car? And the house for sale in that subdivision we passed has our name on it. Usually it's not need that drives us, but simple want. The handbags we own already fill three shelves in the closet; shoe boxes line the others and spread underneath. We have enough jewelry to start a boutique; the house or apartment we live in meets our needs and the car we drive isn't yet paid for. It is from a wellspring of vanity and greed that we seek to acquire more and more. We yield to these desires and in the process fall victim to one Satan's trusted "minions," the god of possession. And before we realize it, our possessions define us and our worth, in our eyes and in the eyes of others. Pride of ownership sets in; the prestige of possessing things beyond what others have and wish they had colors our perceptions of them and of ourselves.

And this evolution brings us to Matthew 6:21. Jesus is in teacher mode in this sermon on a mountain, laying the foundational concepts of the Christian faith that will spring up and spread after his resurrection and ascension into heaven. In the verses preceding verse 21, Jesus warns against storing up earthly treasures that have no eternal value, advising instead that we accumulate heavenly treasures. He calls our attention to the temptation of overvaluing our possessions to the extent that we believe we never have enough. The idea of storing up implies ongoing acquisition. The more we get, the more we want. The now look, the hottest, the most revolutionary, the latest upgrade become must-haves. As the cycle continues, we impose more value on things; they become our treasures. And we do love those things we treasure. As believers we must take Jesus at his word. He is clear that what we store up must not be worldly things that decay or attract unwanted attention from others. Rather, disciples are called to follow Jesus by acquiring heavenly treasures. And what you might ask are "heavenly treasures?" Where do we acquire them? May I suggest the following answers?

Heavenly treasures unlike their earthly counterparts are eternal. They are the treasures we acquire as we grow in right relationship with God; the attributes He gives freely as we seek Him. They spring forth as fruit of His Spirit and are our heart's desire. On the top shelf of the storage closet, Love reigns as the premier heavenly treasure, love of God and His son Jesus Christ. Spoken of in the first commandment: *"Love the Lord thy God with all your heart...,"* it is the heavenly treasure that paves the way to eternity. We crowd the shelf just beneath Love with the heavenly treasure which flows from it—Joy, radiant Joy that is untarnished by any of life's difficulties; in the midst of them, Joy becomes our strength. It is the treasure that pleases God when we lift our voices in songs of joyful praise. Jesus said to his followers, *"Peace I leave with you; my Peace I give you. ...I have told you these things, so that in me you may have peace. In this world you will have trouble. But take heart! I have overcome the world."* Peace, the heavenly treasure given to us by Jesus himself, is the companion of Joy when the storms of life arise. Though the thief may search, he will not find it because it is tucked safely away in the recesses of our heart's storage chest. Patience and Kindness, the twin heavenly treasures, share the corner unit of the storage closet. They are the treasures that enable us to heed Paul's words to the church at Galatia, *"The entire law is summed up in a single command: 'Love your neighbor as yourself.'"* When these heavenly treasures are in abundant supply, we can more easily forgive and live in peace with others. Who will get on our last nerve? Who will drive us to drink? No one! Patience and kindness have that covered. And to add icing to the cake of our heavenly treasures, Goodness, Faithfulness, Gentleness and Self-Control fill any remaining nooks and crannies in the storage unit. These attributes in concert with the other heavenly treasures will guarantee the outcome toward which we strive – to know in our hearts what our treasure is: God and God alone.

15

Do You Believe in Miracles?

You are the God who performs miracles...
              Psalm 77:14

When Jesus stops by and says, "Come, Follow me," our response should be as automatic as it was for the fishermen who first heard the call. Why? Unlike those first responders, we have the benefit of history on our side. We have read the stories of the miracles he performed: healing the sick, restoring sight to the blind, causing the lame to walk again, driving out demonic forces, feeding thousands with the meager contents of a boy's sack lunch, calming a raging sea, raising the dead to life, allowing a man to walk on water. And these are just the stories recorded for posterity. Many more could have been written, but as the Apostle John writes, *"Jesus did many other things as well. If every one of them were written down, I suppose that even the whole world would not have room for the books that would be written."* (John 21:25)

Merriam Webster's Dictionary defines the word miracle as an extraordinary event manifesting divine intervention in human affairs. Every biblical miracle fits that definition. In the years prior to Jesus' sojourn on earth, God himself was the miracle worker. The Old Testament is alive with examples of His divine interventions: the Israelites crossing the Red Sea on dry land to escape the Egyptian army which subsequently drowned when the waters closed upon them; food and water provided over a forty year period as the nation wandered in the desert; the walls of a fortified city crumbling at the blowing of horns and raised voices. As the psalmist proclaims, *"God performs miracles."*

And guess what? He hasn't stopped performing them. Consider just a few of the documented accounts of modern day miracles recorded on oddee.com that speak to God's continuing "intervention in human affairs."

The "mysterious voice" which led police to rescue an 18 month old child who survived for fourteen hours in a car submerged in a Utah river in March 2015. Officer Tyler Bledsoe and other first responders told the CBS affiliate KUTV that they heard a voice from inside the car say clearly, "Help me." And it wasn't, they added, the voice of a child, nor the mother who died upon impact. "It's a miracle," Officer Bledsoe told the news crew.

After giving birth via C-section at Boca Raton Regional Hospital, Ruby Graupera-Cassimiro suffered an amniotic fluid embolism and lapsed into cardiac arrest. For three hours doctors tried to revive her and after 45 minutes without a pulse, they prepared to pronounce her dead. But as they told the family they had done all they could do, Graupera-Cassimiro spontaneously resuscitated. Doctors called her survival a "miracle."

After going missing, 22-month-old Gardell Martin of Mifflinburg, Pennsylvania was found a quarter-mile away from home caught in a tree branch with water gushing around him. He was unconscious. The paramedics arrived and began CPR, which would continue, unbroken, for 101 minutes – in the ambulance, at a community hospital, aboard a medical helicopter and finally in the emergency room of Geisinger Medical Centre. Doctors continued CPR while slowly warming his body temperature which had fallen to 77 degrees. When it reached 82 degrees, they detected a heartbeat. His heart restarted, stunning the doctors and prompting Dr. Maffei, head of the pediatric wing to say he had never encountered such a recovery in his 23 years as a doctor.

And who doesn't recall the dramatic landing of the commercial

Do You Believe in Miracles?

airplane in the Hudson River with the passengers and crew being rescued even as the plane sank into the rigid waters? A print media drawing of the event pictured the plane being carried by a host of angelic like figures, to my mind an accurate interpretation of the Miracle on the Hudson.

On a whim, I surveyed my Facebook friends, asking them to respond to the question, "Do you believe in miracles?" with a simple Yes or No answer. It's not a very scientific survey for sure, but I wanted to get a feel from my social media crowd of their take on the issue. Of the responses so far, only one person said "No." And I'm not surprised. She is an admitted Atheist. The fundamental truth is that to believe in miracles you have to believe the dictionary's definition of the word. And once you do that, it's a small step to belief in God, the divine interventionist. The God who performed miracles in the Old Testament of the Bible is the same God who through his son, Jesus, the Disciples and Apostles performed miracles in the New Testament. And he is the same God who performs miracles today, spectacular interventions as I've noted above, but also in less dramatic fashion in our everyday living. Just reflect for a moment on the prayers you've prayed that have been miraculously answered, not always in the manner you wished, but answered nonetheless; the opportunities that have come your way without explanation or effort; decisions confirmed as right or wrong by the resulting consequences. Only when God is real to you do you understand that miracles happen. In every circumstance of life—the exhilaration of triumphs and the devastation of defeats and everything in between—God is the divine intervention in human affairs. Correct answer to the question: "Yes, I believe in miracles.

16

Filling Station

Now he had to go through Samaria... Jacob's well was there, and Jesus, tired as he was from the journey, sat down by the well... When a Samaritan woman came to draw water, Jesus said to her, "Will you give me a drink?"

John 4:4–7

Back in the day, gas stations were officially called "filling stations." That's what they were designed to do starting in the United States in the early 1900s—fill automobiles with the fuel and lubricants they needed to operate effectively. Though not many people refer to them as such today, their function has not changed. Whether referred to as a gas station or filling station, they are the recognized places to stop in to refuel.

Even further back in the day, circa AD 30 or so, the town well was the recognized place to go for filling water jars necessary for drinking, cooking and washing. Without it, people could not live or function efficiently. The well was in effect the community filling station, not for maintaining vehicles, but the body itself. And as the scripture references, Jacob's well was the place where a tired Jesus stopped to quench His thirst, to fill up with what He needed to continue His journey. In the course of the ensuing conversation between the woman and Jesus, He proclaims that, *"If you knew the gift of God and who it is that asks you for a drink, you would have asked him and he would have given you living water."* (John 4:10)

Filling Station

As their interaction continues, the woman discovers at the well the source of her salvation. It became the place at which she was filled with living water that transformed her life.

We too need a "filling station." We need a place and the time in that place that we set aside faithfully to refuel our spirit, to drink of the living water that quenches the thirst of our souls. We aren't automobiles that can run for days, sometimes weeks without stopping to fill up. To live the life faith demands, we need daily refueling. The practice of beginning the day alone with God in prayer, scripture and reflection, with an open mind to hear a Word from Him is essential to the proper running of our spiritual vehicle. The peace that comes from this practice of spending time in His presence cannot be measured. I know some folk are like the woman at the well; questioning how Jesus was supposed to get water with nothing to draw it with. It's impossible to do. They complain they have too much on their plates already; there's no way they can carve a spot for devotional time in their morning routines. As a former working wife and mother, I can appreciate that argument. It is hard to draw water with no bucket. But where there is a will to do, there is a way. The rewards of setting this quiet time in the morning are worth any sacrifice, and yes, there will be sacrifices: setting the alarm for 5:00 am instead of 5:30; pushing the morning calisthenics to a different time slot; buying an alarm clock sans snooze button; ditching the early morning television shows with their wake-up antics. Trust me though. The reward of this faith discipline will outweigh the value of whatever it replaces.

Just as our cars when properly fueled carry us where we need to go, our spirit, when refreshed with God's word, smooths our passage through the day. Time spent in the place we set aside, the symbolic well from which we draw sustenance, will bring peace, clarity and strength. God's word speaks to our concerns and situations; the devotional materials we read and digest offer insight and encouragement; the conversations—prayers—we speak in these moments of solitude and reflection draw us closer to His will and purposes. Somehow when we've "filled up," the day ahead with its responsibilities and challenges seems less daunting. Our nerves are settled. The "little stuff" doesn't trip us as much and the "big stuff" gets managed with less panic. And this all happens because we discover once the practice of refueling every morning has become a habit that in this quiet time spot, we can surrender to God our plans for the day as we incorporate His fuel to carry us where He wants to go. *"Trust in the Lord with all your heart and lean not to your own understanding. In all your ways acknowledge him and he will direct your path."* (Proverbs 3:5–6) I challenge you to identify your "filling station." And when you've done that, I offer these words of encouragement: At your quiet place, God listens as you talk openly and honestly to Him. There are no concerns you can bring He can't handle. Stories of other believers will strengthen your own resolve to stay the course. His peace will descend upon you and you will leave your "well" in the same spirit as the Samaritan woman – excited to share the good news of the Messiah to those who will listen. Don't let your car be the only thing in your life that gets refueled. Stop daily to fill your soul with living water, the fuel Jesus Christ gives freely.

17

Come to Jesus Moment

Do not be deceived; God is not mocked. A man reaps what he sows. The one who sows to please his sinful nature, from that nature will reap destruction; the one who sows to please the Spirit, from the Spirit will reap eternal life.

Galatians 6:7–8

I declare on this 19th day of June 2015, in light of the terroristic tragedy that unfolded in Charleston, South Carolina that what we have here in the good ole United States is a clear "Come to Jesus Moment."

When a person enters a church, sits with the parishioners for an hour or so during Bible study and then draws a gun and kills nine of them, including the pastor (and speaks racist words of hated during the assault), the time is long past for E and E: plausible excuses and psychological explanations. It's time to "call a s____ a s____" and recognize this act of hatred for what it is—a sin against God and humanity. I refrain from spelling out the idiom considered offensive by many, but the irony of its original meaning can't be over emphasized: to be outspoken, blunt, even to the point of rudeness; to call things by their proper names without "beating around the bush" (Brewer's Dictionary of Phrases and Fable 1913); to explicitly call out something as it is, by its right name without lying, but speaking honestly and directly about a topic and specifically topics that others may avoid due to their sensitivity or the unpleasantness or embarrassing nature of the subject. (Wikipedia.org)

And that is the reality of today. Many of us modern enlightened Christians struggle with the concept of sin. We don't feel comfortable acknowledging that it is sin committed by sinners that brings us to these moments of anguish and despair. Hatred is sin; killing people with no justification other than your hatred of them based upon their race is sin. Promoting racial discord to tear apart neighborhoods and communities is sin. Abusing the authority of your position by killing individuals who have committed no crime is sin. Violence unleashed upon the innocent is sin.

Now I understand why the secular world reacts as it does; to accuse someone of being sinful or to declare certain behaviors or attitudes as sin just isn't done in polite society or over the airwaves (at least on most of them). In the secular world, we say, "I don't understand why he would do such a thing" or "it's difficult to know what drove him to such violence."

But Christians cannot accommodate their faith to the dictates of the culture. And this is what we do when we as Christ followers choose political correctness over bluntness. We must remember that the enemy of our faith is alive and well and cunning, a deceiver of the truth. He artfully twists to his advantage Jesus' command that we "judge not," and has convinced us that the act of pointing to unlawful behaviors or attitudes as sin is judging. But in the largest Christian nation in the world, disciples of Jesus must stand firm in the convictions of our faith. We know sin is real. If it were not, then Jesus died for nothing. Sin is the condition of man. Only when we acknowledge it in ourselves and others, repent, turn from it and whenever possible help others to do the same are we reconciled to God.

And this brings us to our "Come to Jesus" Moment, a time like now when we own the truth that race is as much the defining issue of the 21st century in this country as it was in centuries past; that being truthful about this peculiarity of being an American is a

Come to Jesus Moment

matter we can no longer ignore; that this senseless act of violence and all the other similar acts committed in recent years can be traced to the sin of "not loving our neighbor as ourselves." And if we can't acknowledge the negative impact of our failure to resolve this issue now, when will we? When will we as a Christian nation claim, "No more purposeless killing; no more unwarranted violence; no more race baiting and spewing of hatred over the airwaves or social media? Acknowledging these senseless acts as sin against God and man must drive the conversations in our churches (especially our predominantly white congregations), in our schools, in our homes, in our organizations that claim Christian values, in the legislative halls filled with elected Christians, in all the places where people of faith gather. We know ultimately God is "not mocked", that he will judge the "good, the bad and the ugly." Scripture instructs us to not take revenge, but to leave room for God's wrath; for wrongdoing is His to avenge. (Romans 12:19–20). In the meantime, we do not shy away from acknowledging sin in ourselves or in others. We must hold each other accountable with a spirit of love and mercy, but accountable we must be. We cannot allow the enemy whose goal is the destruction of our faith to continue his assaults. Can this latest sin against humanity in a small African American church be the last such incident to shake this nation's Christian values? Can we not be overcome by evil, but overcome evil with good? Can we turn what the perpetrator meant for evil into something God means for good?

This epiphanic moment requires we acknowledge our failure as people of Christ to address the racial divide and hatred that are a plague in our midst. Oswald Chambers strikes home the point when he writes, "We have to recognize that sin is a fact, not a defect; sin is red-handed mutiny against God… In our mental outlook we have to reconcile ourselves to the fact of sin as the only explanation as to why Jesus Christ came, and as the only explanation of the grief and sorrow in life." (*My Utmost for His Highest*) Though it may seem so, wrong will not remain forever on the throne. Will this horrific act be the turning point that leads to healing and reconciliation? May the history of holocausts in this country and around the world remind us that evil and sin prevail when people of faith and good will remain silent. This is our Come-to-Jesus Moment. My hope, my prayer is that with God's grace we will embrace it.

18

Full-Time Followers

So Elijah went from there and found Elisha son of Shaphat. He was plowing with twelve yoke of oxen, and he himself was driving the twelfth pair. Elijah went up to him and threw his cloak around him. Elisha then left his oxen and ran after Elijah.
I Kings 19:19–20

The chronicle of Elisha's call to ministry as recorded in I Kings 19:19–21 intrigued me for two reasons, the swiftness with which Elisha made the decision to follow the older prophet and the total commitment he gave to that decision. As the scripture reads, Elisha was a simple farmer, engaged in the routine of farming – plowing the fields in preparation for planting. Nothing in the account suggests that after his farming duties were taken care of, he was burning the midnight oil studying the Torah with the hope of one day going into ministry as one of God's prophets. No, until that fateful day Elijah, commanded by God, appeared and threw his cloak around him—the act of anointing, Elisha was a full-time tiller of the soil. But without hesitation, it appears; he dropped the yoke of the plow and his oxen and "ran" after the prophet. To leave the oxen that enabled him to carry out his farming duties was major! Leaving them meant he was done with that line of work; he was committed to the new work that would be required by following Elijah. Verses 20–21 speak to the level of his commitment. He slaughtered the oxen; cooked the meat and fed his family and friends; and burned his plowing equipment! Without doubt his commitment to full time prophetic ministry under Elijah's leadership was sealed.

As 21st century Christ followers, we have New Testament examples revealed in the lives of the disciples and apostles that illustrate what being a full-time believer requires. The matter of swiftness notwithstanding, we see in their lives a commitment to the work of discipleship and carrying out Jesus' Great Commission (Mark 16:15–16 and Matthew 28:16–20). These chronicles define the expectations of "full time" followers. Following Christ is not a part-time endeavor. Christ-likeness is not something we don on Sundays for service or on Wednesday at Bible study. It's not relegated to the weekly choir rehearsal or the monthly committee meeting or church council gathering. When we commit to Jesus, to be His disciple, we can't schedule Him in for selected slots in our calendars. Like Elisha during Old Testament times and the disciples who spread the gospel message following Christ's ascension, our commitment has to be a full-time effort. And herein is the snare so common to us today.

Many of us are more like the rich young man who approached Jesus as recorded in the Gospel of Matthew 19:16–22. He was faultless in his observance of the law. He could check "Yes" to all the markers of obedience to his faith. Yet, despite his seeming righteousness, there was still an area of his life that kept him from becoming a full-time follower. The concept of "slaughtering his oxen and burning his plow" was just too big a commitment. He had a handle on the part-time stuff: murder, adultery, stealing, honoring parents, loving his neighbor. But being a full-time follower required his all, and that was just too difficult for him to surrender. Aren't we the same? We practice the major disciplines of our faith; we are regular worshippers; we participate in service opportunities; we read the Bible and spend as much time as possible in devotion and study; we respond to calls for service in our communities and social organizations. On the outside, we are all right with God. But too often in situations that try our patience, that require overlooking faults, that require sacrifices of time or goods, that stretch our goodwill beyond what we deem necessary, that require our forgiveness for perceived wrongs against us, that move us out of our comfort zones, like the rich young man and unlike Elisha we fail the test of full-time discipleship.

A recent incident in my own life speaks of such failure. A neighbor's teenage granddaughter who had committed a transgression on our property earlier in the year and lied about it came to the front door. She said she wanted to ask my granddaughter a question. I asked if she was the person who had gone into the pool area without permission and she said, "No." This second falsehood was too much! I refused to allow her to come in even when she said she was locked out of the house. I gave her the phone to make a call from the front porch. When she said her grandfather would be home in 15 minutes, I told her she could wait at her house on the porch as that wasn't too long. I admit I was incensed by her lying to my face twice! The next morning as I engaged in my regular devotional time, wouldn't you know the Lord convicted me of not being Christlike in that situation? And He was right! I had been given an opportunity to demonstrate a full-time follower's extension of grace and mercy to someone who had offended me and I blew it big time.

Becoming and continuing to be a full-time follower of Jesus Christ requires a decision and a total commitment to Him. We reflect that commitment as did our ancestors by turning away from our past and giving up everything that might stand in the way of faithfulness to His purposes. We "slaughter our oxen" (our will and our way) and "burn our plows" (the stuff that tethers us to everything not of Christ). Only as we do both are we able to claim full-time status as followers of Jesus Christ.

19

OF DONKEYS & FISH & TEXT MESSAGES

> *The donkey said to Balaam, "am I not your own donkey, which you have always ridden, to this day? Have I been in the habit of doing this to you?" "No," he said.*
>
> Numbers 22:30
>
> *Jonah ran away from the Lord and headed for Tarshish…he found a ship bound for that port…he went aboard and sailed to Tarshish to flee from the Lord. Then the Lord sent a great wind on the sea, and such a violent storm arose that the ship threatened to break up.*
>
> Jonah 1:3–4

I know what you're thinking right about now. Donkeys, Fish, Text Messages. Has that southern sunshine finally taken its toll? Has the old girl lost it? No, quite the opposite in fact; the old girl has this day been blessed with the same divine intervention these two biblical characters knew in their time. Which goes to illustrate that axiom we can trace back to Ecclesiastes 1:9: "there is nothing new under the sun." To be sure we're all on the same page; a little biblical background is in order. Balaam's story is probably the lesser known. He was on his way to a meeting with a king who wanted him to curse God's people, the Israelites. Now Balaam was obedient; he refused to curse the people God said were blessed, but he did agree to meet with the king. On the journey there, his donkey seemed determined to keep him from his rendezvous; first

Of Donkeys & Fish & Text Messages

he turned off the road; secondly, he pressed against a wall to prevent passage and thirdly he lay down under Balaam and refused to move. Each time he delayed the journey, Balaam beat him. Finally, scripture tells us, the Lord opened the mouth of the donkey and he spoke the words quoted above. When Balaam answered, "No," God opened his eyes and he saw the angel of the Lord who had blocked the donkey's passage each time and caused him to behave as he had. Divine intervention – God blocked Balaam's intentions until he understood what the Lord wanted him to do. Most of us know Jonah. In church school we learned he disobeyed God, was swallowed by a great fish and stayed in the fish's belly for three days. Jonah's efforts to avoid doing what God wanted—in this case, to go to the city of Nineveh and preach against it—were spoiled by God's actions. The Lord sent a storm that caused the sailors to toss Jonah into the sea to save them from its fury. And then God provided a huge fish to swallow Jonah so that he would not drown and three days later spit him upon the seashore. Both the raging storm and the great fish were divine interventions in Jonah's life arranged to block his efforts to do something God did not want him to do.

And now we come to my story; a hallelujah moment of divine intervention that proves "there is nothing new under the sun." On my way to the consignment store to drop off a few items, I decided to listen to Pandora on my iPhone. I reached for the car charger in the console; it wasn't there. Immediately I thought back to who had used it last and I recalled that my teenage granddaughter used it on the way from church Sunday. I was annoyed and pulled over to text her. I didn't ask if she had the device; rather I told her she had it and demanded to know where it was! And just to be on the safe side, I decided to send a similar text to my son, the second potential culprit, known to borrow things and not return them in a timely fashion! I pressed Send on my smartphone and waited a moment. Within seconds, the little red icon came up that read the message was not sent. Puzzled, I checked to be sure I had battery life and the Wi-Fi was working. I pressed Send again. And again. And again. And again. Totally frustrated by then, I pulled back into traffic to continue my journey thinking I'd deal with the issue when I got home. Obviously, something was amiss with the smartphone, but I couldn't imagine what. Within a few minutes as I made my turn into the parking lot, the Holy Spirit said, "Remember, you moved the charger from the bottom console area to the little storage pocket on top. The charger is in there." And you guessed it. It was right where I had last placed it. And that's when it hit me! The Lord had divinely blocked the sending of those messages that would have caused hurt feelings and probably anger had they been received. Nothing else can explain why they would not go through. Divine intervention stopped me from a course of action which would not have pleased the Lord. I was deliriously joyful as I realized that the God of yesterday is the same today. For those who know Him as Lord and Savior, He brings about His will and purposes in ways that astonish us, but leave us knowing we serve a God who is real.

A final note: my phone's texting feature is working just fine. Text messages I sent after this divine intervention went right through. Like Balaam and Jonah, I was blinded by my own purposes and those intentions were not God's desire. Because He always knows what is best, He stepped into my situation as He did theirs to achieve His purposes.

20

Are You Serious?

The Lord said to Abram, "Leave your country, your people and your father's household and go to the land I will show you."
                                                                Genesis 12:3

T he Bible is filled with "Are You Serious?" stories. The accounts of God proposing something or doing something that to the human perspective seems out of the ordinary, completely nonsensical, and in some cases just down right ludicrous! Consider the story of Abraham. Called Abram at the time, he was living peaceably and seemingly successfully amongst his people, enjoying life with little design to change anything. And along comes God with what I'm sure was an incredible command. "Leave all this and journey to a place I will show you." (My paraphrase) The biblical account does not suggest that Abram was shocked by this order. But let's face it; he was human. And I can easily believe that his initial response whether verbalized or not was "Are You Serious? Leave my father and family and go where? To someplace you'll show me? Come on; you can't be serious!"

And later on the road to the land to which God was leading him, God must have startled Abraham again when he told him that he and Sarah would give birth to a son. Considering that Abraham and Sarah were old enough to have joined AARP 40 to 50 years earlier, you can understand why the Bible says they laughed at the notion of natural birth. Can't you just hear him chuckling and muttering, "Alright, God, after all these years. We just celebrated my 100th birthday and Sarah is 90! "Are you serious?"

The Bible records only the actions of brothers Simon Peter and Andrew, James and John when Jesus said to them, "Come, follow me." Maybe the chance to get away from the drudgery of fishing for a living was incentive enough. We don't really know. But seemingly without a backwards glance the brothers fall in step with the Savior. But what must have been the response of the father sitting there under the Zebedee and Sons Fishing sign busily preparing the nets for the day's work? Out of the blue with no warning, Jesus walks by and calls to his sons and they leave without a word. (At least the Bible doesn't record any.) Realizing that his work force has been reduced to one, he would not be faulted for shouting after them, "Hey. Where are you guys going? What's going on? Are you serious?"

I could go on and on with these biblical examples of "Are You Serious?" moments. What I'm hoping is clear that these unexpected, perhaps crazy moments serve to make us more receptive to God's purposes. They reveal who God is and how He orchestrates who we are and who He wants us to be. Recently I read the story of Katie Davis, the young woman from Nashville, Tennessee, whose decision to do mission work at an orphanage in Uganda rather than attend college must certainly have been an "Are you serious?" moment for her parents. But for Katie, God was shaping His purposes in what seemed unconventional at the time. In the years that followed, the Amazima Ministries she founded has continued to serve the needs of underprivileged children and families. And just as importantly, she teaches and shares the Good News of the Gospel to all who will listen.

Perhaps you too have known persons whose ideas were just too risky, too outside the box, too unorthodox. And probably in those moments you either thought or voiced "Are you serious?" when they shared their plans with you. But in time as those ideas bore fruit you realized more was at work than first met the eye. Let's conclude with the biblical account of one Simon of Cyrene. You may recall he was the traveler in town on the day Jesus was crucified. The scripture reads, *"They seized Simon from Cyrene who was on his way in from the country, and put the cross on him and made him carry it behind Jesus."* (Luke 23:26) Though the Bible doesn't give us any hint of Simon's initial reaction, it's not hard to imagine his first thoughts were akin to "What? Are you serious? I just got to town; I don't even know what's going on. Who is this man anyway? What crime has he committed? And why do I have to help him carry this cross?" Simon had no idea that his part in the crucifixion story would still be told some 2000 plus years later. I think what he did, even if forced to do it, speaks a message to us today.

Like him we live and go about our daily routines not expecting to play a major part in God's design for His creation. But we do. Some of them we take on willingly; others we are forced to accept as part of someone else's agenda. No matter how we arrive at the juncture, we are given the opportunity to do the unexpected or to make a difference by taking that very action that makes others respond, "Are you serious? You're really going on a mission trip? You're volunteering at a shelter in that part of town? You're going to adopt a child now? You're starting your own business?"

Simon realized that the soldiers were serious; he shouldered the cross and followed Jesus to Calvary. When we embrace the "Are you serious?" moments that God orchestrates in our lives and see in them His call, we respond and follow Him, not to Calvary but to Eternity.

Part Two

Faith: Profession/Possession?

As Jesus went on from there, two blind men followed him, calling out, "Have mercy on us Son of David!" When he had gone indoors, the blind men came to him, and he asked them, "Do you believe that I am able to do this?" "Yes, Lord," they replied. Then he touched their eyes and said, "According to your faith it will be done to you"; and their sight was restored.
Matthew 9:27–30

Is faith something we simply profess or something we possess? For Christians, it's a valid query. We make a profession of faith when we accept Jesus Christ as the Son of God who died for our transgressions and rose for our redemption. To make a profession is as defined by Webster's Dictionary, "the act of taking the vows of a religious community; an act of publicly claiming a belief, faith or opinion." Though it may take a measure of courage, publicly professing faith, usually to join a church, is rather commonplace. But profession is not sufficient over the long haul. At some point after the simple declaration must come the realization that faith is more than something you speak, it is something you must possess.

All too often we easily wear the mantle of faith; when life is running smoothly with no major concerns, perhaps a few annoyances now and then, but nothing we can't handle ourselves, our faith is a profession, not a possession. The truth is we can't know what it means to possess faith until we have life experiences that demand

Faith: Profession/Possession?

the exercise of it. And we only come to that state when things are off kilter; when hard knocks have bowled us over and we land in desperation on our knees. That was pretty much the state of the blind men. Scripture doesn't tell us much about them; only that they were blind and followed Jesus after He had healed a ruler's daughter. We can surmise that they were among the onlookers and heard what He had done; raised a girl from death to life! Whether or not they had professed belief in Him as God's Son prior to this is unknown. What we do know is that they possessed faith enough in Him to answer in the affirmative when Jesus asked if they believed He could heal their blindness.

Difficult, desperate times force us to move from profession to possession of faith. We understand profession is not enough. We need something more, something to which we can cling. That something is faith, the first commodity of the triune: faith, hope and love. When faith is a possession, it takes up residence inside us; no longer just a generic word spoken lightly in religious circles. When we possess faith, it helps us deal with the realities of our circumstances; it keeps us moving forward; it sustains us; it enables us to make sense of the nonsensical. Faith that is a possession says, "Hold on," when the rope we grasp is frayed and begins to slip from our fingers. Faith that is a possession defines who we are no matter what our situation. Faith that is a possession helps us endure the unendurable. It makes the impossible possible. Just ask the two blind men. Their response, "Yes, Lord," affirmed their faith. And because they possessed it, Jesus could say unto them, *"According to your faith will it be done to you."* (Matthew 9:29) The lesson for us is simple. Our faith must be more than a profession; it must mimic that of our biblical ancestors and others who never stopped believing and who never gave up hope, demonstrating that their faith was their possession, and not just a profession of belief.

2

Practice Makes the Difference

"Do not let your hearts be troubled…"

John 14:1

I think it's true what Oswald Chambers says, "The crisis will reveal whether we have been practicing or not." In some ways it's an elementary concept; one common to the human experience. If we don't practice regularly the lessons we are taught in school, at exam time (for some a certain crisis situation), we do not pass the test. If we learn to drive with little real road experiences, we don't know what to do when a potential crisis looms on the road ahead of us.

In the spiritual realm to which Mr. Chambers alludes, practicing the principles of our faith is required if we are to meet the challenges life brings. This test of our discipleship does not occur when life is moving smoothly, without conflict, chaos or confusion. After all, what is there to test during periods of calm and prosperity? Not until the crisis erupts does the testing begin, intrusive and unrelenting. It is in these moments that we discover whether our preparation has merit. Few crisis situations allow "cram time" or hurried last minute getting ready strategies. No, the crisis happens and either we are prepared or not. Those believers who in their non-crisis hours give deliberate attention to the disciplines of discipleship: prayer, reflection, Bible study, devotional time, stillness before the Lord, praise and worship will be the ones prepared for a crisis. They do not falter or lose hope. They know the Lord is gently leading them through the test, no matter how painful it may be.

We see the truth of this concept when we reflect upon the reactions of the family and friends of the nine victims slain in the African Methodist Episcopal church on June 17, 2015 in Charleston, NC. The crisis revealed to the world what it means for believers who are steadfast in the disciplines of their faith to face the unthinkable. The words of forgiveness they uttered; the strength they demonstrated; the trust in God their actions spoke. There was no rancor, no calls for retaliation. Their years of "practice" made the difference in their response to a tragedy that shook the nation. They knew God was gently leading them through the crisis, no matter how painful it was.

We followers of Christ understand why Jesus spoke those words to the Disciples; in addition to offering them comfort about his impending departure, He wanted them to know that periods would come when they would be troubled. The words ring true today. We can easily fall victim to worry, anxiety and fear, most especially in circumstances like the one in Charleston. And in less traumatic situations, we can cower fearfully when we have not been consistent in practicing the tenets of the faith we profess. Those practices build over time the spiritual DNA that sustains us. They enable us to be guided by the concluding words of the verse, "Trust in God; trust also in me." (James 14:1) Trusting in God is the foundation of our faith. His comfort, consolation and courage are the fruits of that trust. And the ability to trust without fear or anxiety propels us when the crisis strikes.

3

Heard From the Lord Today?

"And the word of the Lord came to him: 'What are you doing here, Elijah?'"

I Kings 19:9

Suppose someone asked you, "Have you heard God's voice today?" What would be your likely answer? An automatic, "No." A hedged, "Not yet." An evasive, "What do you mean, have I heard His voice?" A defensive, "Have you?" It's a question well aimed at professed Christian believers. And because we profess our belief in Him and His word, the question should not cause any consternation. But as the possible answers indicate, it just might.

Not many of us today claim to hear God's word as did the prophets in biblical times. The Old Testament is filled with examples of God speaking directly to those He called: The Lord said to Abram, *"Leave your country, your people and your father's household and go to the land I will show you."* (Genesis 12:1) *"Moses! Moses! ... I have seen the misery of my people in Egypt... So now, go. I am sending you to Pharaoh to bring the Israelites out of Egypt."* (Exodus 3:7–10) There are so many instances of God speaking to His people in those days that hearing from Him seemed almost commonplace. Not only did they hear from Him when He had a specific task for them, but He spoke when they were at their weakest as was Elijah in the scripture referenced above. Threatened with death by Queen Jezebel, Elijah was terrified; in fear he fled for his life.

Totally exhausted he pleaded with God to let him die. We can understand his desperation; sometimes we feel like that. Trials, tribulations abound. Everywhere we turn it seems we are under attack. And even when we remember that our Savior endured more than anyone of us ever will, it's still hard. Those on the sidelines who jeered Him as He hung on the cross, taunting Him to save Himself if He was the Son of God are with us today. They are the ones who say, "Where is God in all this? You do all that praying and worshipping and you're still going through that. What's the point of your faith?"

The psalmist's refrain: *"Why are you downcast, O my soul? Why so disturbed within me? Put your hope in God, for I will yet praise him, my Savior and my God."* (Psalm 42:5, 11) reminds us that we are to press through the agonies and challenges by remembering in whom we have placed our hope and trust. And even though the Lord may not come to us at the mouth of a cave to ask in essence, "What's wrong? Why are you here?" we hear His voice in other ways. A devotional piece we read may bring His voice to us loudly and clearly as someone else's thoughts speak to our need of the moment.

Oftentimes we hear God's voice in the words or actions of others: family, friends or strangers. Recall the time when someone said or did something that spoke to your needs without a word from you. And of course, when we open our Bibles He speaks to us through page after page of His inspired word. Opening the Bible is akin to slipping a CD into a disc player and listening to your favorite song. When you open God's word, His word leaps from the pages and in them you hear His voice. He speaks to your situation. As with Elijah, He allows your moment of despair, but then He gives through His word, the course of action He desires for you. You have but to be still and hear. He speaks love and joy and comfort and peace. He reminds you His grace is more than sufficient for whatever you are going through.

If you will but listen, you will hear. And if anyone is audacious enough to ask, "Have you heard from the Lord today?" Look them in the eye and say, "Shh; the Lord is talking to me right now."

4

Topsy-Turvy

"...These men who have turned the world upside down have come here also..."

Acts 17:6

The Jews and rabble rousers were furious! They searched the neighborhood, street by street, looking for the apostles Paul and Silas who for three weeks had shared the good news of the gospel in the local synagogue and caused many to become believers. In their fury at not finding them, they drug Jason and others from the house in which the apostles were known to have stayed. And before the city officials, they accused these "scapegoats" of harboring "these men who have turned the world upside down," i.e. "topsy turvy." As the Jesus movement, propelled by the apostles, continued to grow and move throughout the regions it had that kind of impact upon the world. Touched by the message of salvation and hope, those who accepted found their lives radically changed. Suddenly the status quo just wasn't enough anymore.

This idea of believers in Jesus Christ turning the world upside down is not relegated to biblical history. God expects us today to still be those about whom such words are spoken. As contemporary Christians, we ought to be turning the world topsy-turvy. Our peculiar witness should manifest itself in ways that run counter to the commonly accepted norms of our times. This is not the time to be "secret disciples," like Joseph of Arimathea, a disciple of Jesus, but secretly because he feared the Jews. (John 19:38). He hid his faith, living in fear of exposure. Willing to embrace Jesus' teachings away from the public eye, he was unwilling to face the possible consequences of open discipleship. Discipleship requires us to examine everything in the revealing light of our faith. Are our relationships any different than those of folk who do not claim Christ as Lord? Do we fear rejection by nonbelievers who are part of our secular circles? And because of that fear remain silent when the secular bumps head with the sacred? Do the practices in our homes reflect our faith or are they quite similar to those of the neighbors who make no pretense of their worship of false gods? Ever notice how vocal the nonbelievers are; seldom is there any hesitation in their declarations. Is there any distinction in followers of Jesus in the workplace? Are our actions and conversations markers of our faith? Or do we tread lightly, fearful of ridicule or worse? And what about our use of leisure time? Is it an example to others of what Christ demands of those who claim his name? Or do we lodge our beliefs in "Faith Daycare" while we enjoy fun in the sun, the seven day cruise or the excitement of a Las Vegas weekend? In other words, do we take a vacation from our faith because we're on vacation!

In these situations of daily living, our Lord offers us the same opportunity to choose as He did the apostles and followers in biblical times. We can join the rabble rousers who disdain the gospel message and seek ways to discredit it. We can choose the wide path on which everyone else is walking or we can be like Paul and Silas and the other carriers of the gospel. We can take the road that disrupts the status quo, the one that forces confrontation with the earthly pretender. We can on that road led by the Holy Spirit live our professional and personal lives in ways that glorify God. And in so doing, we can bring turmoil to the complacency of our times by the bold witness of the same gospel that stirred the people over two thousand years ago. We can be Status Quo Confronters who live in such a way that upside down, topsy-turvy is the preferred choice.

5

SUBSTITUTING 101

He himself bore our sins in his body on the tree, so that we might die to sins and live for righteousness; by his wounds you have been healed.

I Peter 2:24

As a retired secondary school educator, I know well the role of the "substitute." In the hallowed halls of learning, these are the stalwart individuals who assume the role and responsibilities of the teacher who is out of service for the day. Getting the call to duty, often on short notice, the substitute enters the classroom door to greet students who are not always receptive. Many are deliberately uncooperative and others spend the class period devising ways to torment the stand-in. It is not often a job that brings joy. Sometimes there is a lesson plan; other times there is not. Students try all kinds of antics to avoid doing anything of substance for that period. Yet having accepted the responsibility of standing in for the regular teacher, substitutes carry on, assuming the call and duty in good faith.

As I read Peter's words in the scripture above, I realized that long before the concept of "substituting" entered the lexicon of educational practices, Jesus had demonstrated what it means to really be a substitute. With His shouldering the cross and climbing the hill to Golgotha, He became the ultimate definition of the word. He had no need of a lesson plan for the task He chose to complete;

He was the lesson plan. Willingly, as our substitute, He bore our responsibilities, or more accurately, our inability to shoulder our responsibilities. He stood in for us and not for just a day or two or three, but for eternity. His sacrifice on the cross modeled what it means to do the work for someone who is not able to complete that work for himself. Years of human disobedience and antics that tried the Lord's patience required a more perfect work be done. When the teacher is absent, the work done by the substitute may or may not meet the regular teacher's standards. But Jesus's substitution exceeded the work required by the law. He, who was without sin, took mankind's sins upon himself and paid the price for those sins with His life.

Such a substitution boggles the mind, humbles us and should reduce us to a state of complete subjugation to Him, the Master Sub. To reconcile humankind with God the Father, Jesus answered the call. In fact, long before we even knew we would need a substitute, He was ready and waiting for the call. And unlike the school substitute who assumes the role as teacher and takes over expecting to be compensated for that work, our Savior knew there would be no pay warrant for Him when he uttered, "It is finished." Willingly He waived the cost and served that stint on the cross in full knowledge that He was a stand in for us who deserved to be there. No school substitute works for free; but that is exactly what Jesus did. Freely without reservation, He gave his life on the cross that the world might be saved. Facing a crowd of unreceptive faces, He pressed on to achieve the purpose to which He had been called. Is there anyone better to follow than the one who paved the way to eternity by subbing for us on the cross? I don't think so.

6

HE FEELS YOUR PAIN

John was beheaded in the prison... Now when Jesus heard this, he withdrew from there in a boat to a deserted place by himself.
                                              Matthew 14:10–13
When Jesus saw her weeping, he was greatly disturbed in spirit and deeply moved... Jesus wept.
                                              John 11:33–35

The picture of my baby brother, fifteen years my junior, last born of the family of nine children in a hospital gown, gingerly eating make my heart ache. So do the photos of him with other siblings at a family gathering—gaunt of face, extremely thin, smile forced. They make tears form behind my eyes and the hollow feeling inside grow. Years of unhealthy lifestyle choices have taken their toll; liver and kidneys are in full rebellion. I send my usual text: "praying." And I am, even as I wonder if prayer is enough. What else can I do? After all I'm the big sister, the oldest, with a rep for being spiritual. As I carry him in my thoughts throughout the day, whispering prayers for his healing, I remember his plight and my response to this season of his life are not unfamiliar to my Savior. The glimpses of Jesus in the scriptures above as Son of God and Son of Man are affirmations for us. How comforting to know that His divinity did not separate Him from those He came to save then; it does not separate Him from us today.

His very incarnation allowed our Lord to know firsthand the agony, misery and pain of human existence. We may be tempted to think in times like this that there is no way He understands the heartache of humanity; that because of His divinity, He would be above it, consigned to the celestial domain of observation devoid of feeling.

But that was not God's plan. In an ultimate, matchless expression of love, God fashioned His son to feel the same anguish we feel when life is rocky and hard and devastating. The scriptures above attest to the affect deaths of loved ones and close friends had on Him. Like us He was sorrowful; He withdrew; He was disturbed in spirit; He cried. He sought solitude in which to process His grief. We imagine that like us in our "prayer closet," He cried out to God in prayer in these moments. The fact of His divinity notwithstanding, His humanity offers assurance that He understands. He has been where we are. He has walked in our shoes. He has felt what we feel. How comforting to know then, that it is Jesus who sits at the right hand of God, the Father, interceding on our behalf. It is Jesus who shepherds us through our circumstances. It is Jesus who right now knows all about my baby brother. We serve a Savior who as Son of Man has been there and done that (and yes, probably has a heavenly cap and t-shirt proclaiming the same); and as Son of God has everything my baby brother needs.

I'm back to the beginning now. What as big sister can I do? What as big sister am I supposed to do? Nothing in the human for sure. In God's power and by his grace, I can and will continue to circle this precious brother of mine in prayer. I will trust that God is in control and know I am not. I will lift his name and his need for healing in earnest petition. I will believe in the miracle of prayer. I will trust that God hears my prayers and will answer them. And finally I will be at peace that God knows best; that the answer to my prayer is forthcoming and though it may not take the form I envision, it will be God's best answer because that's all He gives. And no matter what, I will praise Him for my brother's life and live my faith in thanksgiving for all He has done, is doing and has yet to do in it. (May 30, 2015)

7

Automatic Praise

At this, Job got up and tore his robe and shaved his head. Then he fell to the ground in worship and said, "Naked I came from my mother's womb, and naked will I depart. The Lord gave and the Lord has taken away; may the name of the Lord be praised."
Job 1:20–22

Not many of us modern day Christians can offer such a testimony of faith. To worship and praise God at the moment when disaster strikes requires more than most can muster. Yet Job, without even knowing Jesus Christ and His gift of salvation, behaved as though he did. When news of the loss of his children and his property assailed him, he demonstrated how the faithful are called to respond when the bombshells of life explode. Tearing one's robe and shaving the head were ancient ways of expressing grief and sorrow. We do something similar when we don black attire, veil our faces or wear dark glasses to hide our tears. By these actions we show that we are human as Job did when disaster struck.

But here's the difference. Notice what Job did after altering his appearance to signify his sorrow. He fell to the ground and worshipped God. In that worship posture, he acknowledged the truth of man's relationship to God: everything he had, God had given so it was within God's power to do with what He gives as He so pleased. And then Job did what few manage; he actually praised God in the throes of his acute sorrow and heartache.

Verse 22 tells us that Job did not sin by accusing God of any wrongdoing.

Amazing, isn't it? If you like I have been where Job found himself—in the deepest of despair caused by the loss of something or someone precious – you know how difficult it is to emulate his actions. Even though we claim Jesus Christ as our Savior and expect if we are obedient, to live with Him in eternity one day, nonetheless when disaster like this occurs, our first response sadly is not that of worship and praise. Mine was not when my husband died unexpectedly, before I could even say good-bye. One minute he was fine and in the next it seems, gone from me forever. I wish I could have been like Job. I ought to have been more like him. Instead of bewilderment and wails of "Why, Lord why," I should have fallen on my knees, not in supplication for reversal of God's decision, but in praise and thanksgiving for what He had given and now chose to take back for His good reasons. A song of praise should have accompanied the flow of tears from my eyes.

Alas; I was no Job that night. I know the Lord would have preferred a more "Job like" behavior, probably expected it from someone who claimed to be His disciple. Thankfully I serve a Savior who is both loving and merciful and understands our human frailties. Over and over again, He gives us second chances to grow into the believer He created. Our friend Job was one of a kind, even for his day. His actions are still worthy of imitation, even more so now that we know the full story. Jesus has come, paid the price for our sins and will come again to claim us as His own. Because of this surety, we have every reason to worship and to praise no matter the circumstances of our lives. And to do it from the moment disaster strikes.

8

Ethical Infants

"No one knows about that day or hour, not even the angles in heaven, nor the Son, but only the Father... Therefore keep watch because you do not know on what day your Lord will come... So you must be ready, because the Son of Man will come at an hour when you do not expect him."

Matthew 24:36–44

During my devotional time, I was struck by a statement reportedly made in 1948 by General Omar Bradley: "We have grasped the mystery of the atom and rejected the Sermon on the Mount... Ours is a world of nuclear giants and ethical infants." Yes, I thought, that kind of sums up who and what we have become in our time—colossus in our scientific understandings; nascent in the spiritual realms. As I continued with the New Testament reading for the day, I realized that the general's assessment is not just global in its perspective; it's personal also, especially when we consider Jesus' words in the gospel writing of Matthew.

How are the two proclamations related? Consider for a moment the technological advances of our day and how much attention we accord them. The majority of us delight in the latest gadgets and internet resources. From young to old we have become wizards in the use all technology offers for both work and leisure time. We fret if our children aren't introduced quickly enough to the art of all things technological so that they aren't left behind in the digital age.

In the frenzy to stay current, to be informed, to master the very latest of this secular preoccupation with all things technological, it is easy to lose sight of what faith teaches. Our religious resource book, The Bible, tells us in Jesus' words that we are to keep watch in how we live because we do not know the day in which the Lord will return. His admonition suggests it is wise to be ready at all times, since His return will occur when we don't expect Him. How foolish we are if we've become so mesmerized by the technological wizardry of the day that we neglect the things of lasting value, i.e. the tenets of our faith and how that faith calls us to live. We must resist the temptation of being technically astute at the cost of neglecting to live as followers of Jesus Christ. When the Son of Man returns, He will not care how savvy we are on the computer or how competent we've become in using the internet or how we've mastered the intricacies of our smartphones. His command to be "ready" when He comes will not be demonstrated in those attributes.

On the contrary, being ready as He expects us to be as His followers will mean we are engaged in carrying out His commandments, involved in those aspects of life on earth that point to Him and demonstrate our maturity as Christians. Others may wrap themselves in the robes of scientific, technological prowess, but disciples will be clothed in garments that uphold and display what the Master teaches in His word. Secure in His truth alone, disciples will be about His business, finding their power and accomplishment in Him alone, not in the technology that has the potential to stunt, even destroy our spiritual growth, and subsequent eternity with Him.

9

The Least Likely Source

Meanwhile, Saul was still breathing out murderous threats against the Lord's disciples. He went to the high priest and asked him for letters to the synagogues in Damascus, so that if he found any there who belonged to the Way, whether men or women, he might take them as prisoners to Jerusalem.

Acts 9:1–2

Last evening after watching one of those international government conspiracy movies replete with the indiscriminate violence that drives the action when the good guy challenges the despicable bad guy, I decided that a believer can mine nuggets of wisdom from the least likely sources. As the film rolled toward its gripping conclusion, the good guy finally confronts one of the villains in an effort to convince him to betray his cohorts for the good of the world. With absolute grim seriousness he says to the elder conspirator, "Sometimes a man meets his destiny on the road he took to avoid it." The words resonated with me such that I jumped up and grabbed a Post-it pad as I thought, "that succinctly captures the Apostle Paul's experience."

We of the faith know his story. Saul (as he was named) knew his destiny; he fervently persecuted the followers of Jesus and watched in silence as a crowd stoned to death Stephen, one of Jesus' disciples. With the approval and even encouragement of the Jewish elders, high priests and authorities of the time, Saul was a rising star in the movement to stamp out the "heresy" of the followers of the Way. Never would it have entered his mind that the course he pursued was anything less than the destiny that was his by right of birth, education and Roman citizenship. Oh, but the God we serve is no hostage to man's sense of his destiny. The very roads we avoid as having no part in our future are often the ones God brings us to and sets us upon. Just ask Saul/Paul.

Meanwhile, Saul was still breathing out murderous threats against the Lord's disciples… As he neared Damascus on his journey, suddenly a light from heaven flashed around him. He fell to the ground and heard a voice say to him, *"Saul, Saul, why do you persecute me?" "Who are you, Lord?" Saul asked. "I am Jesus, whom you are persecuting,"* he replied. *"Now get up and go into the city, and you will be told what you must do."* (Acts 9:1–6) On that road to Damascus Saul/Paul met his destiny. It wasn't the destiny upon which he had set his sights; at all costs he would have avoided betraying the cause he championed so fiercely. At the time though he did not realize God's plan for his salvation would stop him dead in his tracks, that his destiny was not linked to the destruction of the Christian faith, but to the preaching and witnessing of it throughout the Gentile world.

How powerful is the Word of the Lord that even in the run of the mill experiences, if we listen closely enough, we can hear still hear His voice. In a film rated R for its violence, someone wrote into the script words for us to ponder. As disciples of Jesus Christ, we may too find our way to His purposes in the most unlikely places, and on roads we never might have traveled otherwise. May we be so attuned to His voice on the journey that His word never escapes our hearing; and may we be on the lookout for the smallest kernels of His wisdom in each of our experiences.

10

LIVING LIKE JESUS

Then Jesus came to them and said, "All authority in heaven and on earth has been given to me. Therefore go and make disciples of all nations, baptizing them in the name of the Father and of the Son and of the Holy Spirit, and teaching them to obey everything I have commanded you..."

Matthew 28:18–19

He said to them, "Go into all the world and preach the good news to all creation. Whoever believes and is baptized will be saved, but whoever does not believe will be condemned."

Mark 16:15–16

How can we of the 21st century live like Jesus? Is that even possible? Was Jesus' Great Commission noted above just a mandate for His disciples? Or is it relevant for us today? Fascinating questions of faith! They are valid questions too; ones we dare not brush aside if we are to realize the prize for which we proclaim we strive: eternity with the Savior. How do we understand how Jesus lived? Reflection upon both His words and His deeds reveals all we need know. Yes, it's true; His was an agrarian society totally different than the industrialized, militarized, technology-striven world in which we live now.

But despite these differences, I believe we can choose to live as He did, or not.

Jesus was humble, not proud or arrogant or self-seeking. Jesus walked among and touched in positive, uplifting ways the lives of the lost, the least and the last. Jesus resisted the cultural temptations of His time by keeping His focus on His purpose for living. Jesus never took credit for any of His successes; He gave all credit to God. Jesus did not seek His own comfort, nor did He value material possessions. Jesus' total allegiance and obedience were to God.

Jesus always prayed.

That kind of lifestyle is possible, no matter the century. Imitating Jesus in each of these areas is a matter of choice. If we desire to live like him, we make these attributes of His character a reality in our own lives. Will that mean we may be misunderstood, shunned, unappreciated, denied what is rightfully ours, persecuted, held back, overlooked, relegated to the sidelines of life? Yes, that is exactly what it may mean. But these backlashes for living like Jesus don't mean we can't. It means we choose to or not.

The Great Commission is the definitive instruction Jesus left with the believers. It continues to be His premier word to us today. Sharing the good news of the gospel and obeying Jesus' teachings are the hallmarks of our faith. No time boundary keeps us from this calling. Jesus expects us to be as powerful witnesses to who He is and what He has done for us as were our biblical ancestors.

11

FRIGHTENING WORDS!

"Send them from my presence! Let them go!
Jeremiah 15:1

I shuddered as I completed reading chapters 12 through 15:1 in the book of Jeremiah. When the Lord gets His dander up, watch out! Poor Jeremiah had the unenviable task of telling the people of Jerusalem that God had had enough of their disobedience. He was as we might say in the popular vernacular, "too through with them." All too soon, they would suffer awful consequences for their continuing sinfulness. At the pronouncement of what their future held in store, the people understandably were afraid. And what do you think they did? I'm glad you asked. They did exactly what we ourselves do when we mess up and are frightened of the consequences of our actions; they cried out to God to save them! "O Lord," they prayed, "we acknowledge our wickedness and the guilt of our fathers; we have indeed sinned against you." Or as we might intone today, "Lord, I'm sorry. If you'll just get me out this mess and save me, I promise I will go back to church; I will read my Bible more often and I will pray every day!" But according to the Scriptures, God did not relent; on the contrary, He spoke to Jeremiah words that are akin to giving someone the outstretched "talk to the hand gesture" in our times: *"Even if Moses or Samuel were to stand before me, my heart would not go out to these people. Send them away from my presence! Let them go!"*

This is the response that prompted my shudder and made me say out loud, "Thank God for His Son Jesus!" For if Jesus had not come to earth to live and preach and heal and teach and eventually die on Calvary's cross, we would be lost, without hope and subject to the consequences of God's wrath as were our biblical ancestors. In all honesty, we are no different than them. Our disobedience displeases Him. And despite our belief that He loves us and is faithful to His promises to us, we continue in our willfulness and sinfulness. He asks of us obedience to His teachings and commandments, but like our faith ancestors we are hard headed. We go our own way, ignoring God and His claim upon our lives. And when He allows our stubbornness to determine our paths and we find ourselves lost again, we recover sufficiently from our faith amnesia to remember Him. It is then in despair we seek His forgiveness and salvation. That's why I utter, "Thank you Jesus." It is only by His sacrifice on the cross that our sins are covered.

But even as I speak the words, I remember that though Jesus secured our salvation for us by His ultimate sacrifice, we are still held accountable for how we live our lives. Grace is not cheap; Christ died that we might receive it. At that "great gettin' up morning," we will bow before Jesus and there be rewarded accordingly for our obedience or not. We who have had the gospel of Jesus Christ to guide our journey will be unable to offer any excuse. And sadly some of us will hear Him say one last time, *"Send them away from my presence! Then they will go away to eternal punishment, but the righteous to eternal life."* (Matthew 25:46)

12

Sanctuary

Who shall separate us from the love of Christ? Shall trouble or hardship or persecution or famine or nakedness or danger or sword? ... No, in all these things we are more than conquerors through him who loved us. For I am convinced that neither death nor life, neither angels nor demons, neither the present nor the future, nor any powers, neither height nor depth nor anything else in all creation, will be able to separate us from the love of God that is in Christ Jesus our Lord.

Romans 8:35–39

The challenge churns your insides. The crisis cripples your faith response. The dilemma destroys your confidence and worry takes up residence in your spirit. "Where are you, O God? Now that I desperately need you, where are you?" Let's stop, step back for a moment and refocus. Jesus Christ, our Savior, our help in times of trouble, our all and all, has not deserted or abandoned us to the vicissitudes of life. When He chose to come down from the Mount of Transfiguration as recorded in Matthew, chapter 17: *"After six days Jesus took with him Peter, James and John the brother of James, and led them up a high mountain by themselves. There he was transformed before them. His face shone like the sun, and his clothes became white as the light ... But Jesus came and touched them. 'Get up', he said ...As they were coming down the mountain Jesus instructed them...,"* He demonstrated His commitment to stay with us on the journey up and through eternity. He could have decided differently and accompanied Moses and Elijah back to Heaven; after all, by this time in His ministry He'd accomplished much: miraculous healings, sermons and parabolic homilies, completed basic training for His twelve disciples, fed thousands with the scantiest of resources, destroyed demonic forces, and challenged the religious leaders and their hypocritical leadership. But He didn't. He stayed until it was time for His crucifixion and resurrection; and in so doing He modeled for us how we don't give up the fight no matter how desperate our situations seem to be.

In coming down the mountain to resume the work He came to do, Jesus issued each of us what I term a divine insurance policy, a sanctuary that protects us from worry and fear. In the midst of our human condition, Jesus' descent continues to offer comfort and peace and answer that question, "Where are you, Lord?" He and His actions say clearly, "I am here. Do not worry; trust me. I am all you need to make it through." The Bible overflows with words of assurance that provide the sanctuary our souls seek: *"I lift up my eyes unto the hills – where does my help come from? My help comes from the Lord, the Maker of heaven and earth."* (Psalm 121:1–2); *"The Lord is my light and my salvation—whom shall I fear? The Lord is the stronghold of my life—of whom shall I be afraid?"* (Psalm 27:1) and that most often recited, *"He who dwells in the shelter of the Most High will rest in the shadow of the Almighty. I will say of the Lord, 'He is my refuge and my fortress, my God in whom I trust. ...Because he loves me, says the Lord, I will rescue him..."* (Psalm 91:1–2, 14)

It's simple really. We face the challenges, the crises, and the impossible dilemmas of the human condition in the best way possible for those who believe in the power of Jesus and the power of the Cross. We seek sanctuary in the word of God as recorded in the Bible. Within the pages of this divinely inspired insurance policy, we hear His gentle whispers, bask in His promises and find strength to stay the course with confidence and courage.

13

DUALITY OF FAITH

"Do not love the world or anything in the world. If anyone loves the world, the love of the Father is not in him. For everything in the world – the cravings of sinful man, the lusts of the eyes and the boasting of what he has and does – comes not from the Father but from the world."

I John 2:15–16

I saw the faith-based movie, **War Room**, yesterday. Christians are flocking to it as a "must see" for all who claim Jesus Christ as Savior. It is a thoughtful production that emphasizes the power of prayer, the weapon of choice for the faithful. But the take home line for me was the comment the seasoned-saint made to the police officers as they wrote their report of an attempted robbery in which she and the other main female character were the intended victims. Rather than surrender her purse as the robber demanded, she responded boldly and firmly, "No! In the name of Jesus, drop that knife." The scene ends with the bad guy staring in bafflement at his potential victims; and in the next scene the policemen struggle to understand what happened and even more so to record it correctly. When one of them repeats her statement, she tells him to be sure to "Put Jesus in there. I said in the name of Jesus. That's what's wrong with the world today; always leaving Jesus out." And that to me was the message of the day.

Too often in our daily living, our homes, our places of work and recreation and even in our churches, we "leave Jesus out." I suspect this happens because we have allowed our faith to straddle the divide between the natural or material and the spiritual—the secular and the sacred. I further suspect that because we allow it in our places of worship, we accept it as the norm in all the other places we move and have our being. Think for a moment of the myriad of church activities that are actually secular in design, in tone, in purpose but have been incorporated into the community of faith as a ministry of the church; novel, cutting edge ideas that we ourselves generate with little or no guidance from the Holy Spirit. Such practices allow us to sanction as sacred or holy that which is not. Because we "leave Jesus out," we undertake ministries that are not informed by God's will and purposes; ministries not necessarily bad or evil in and of themselves, but lacking scriptural foundation nonetheless. And let's be real. If within our faith community, we have not the model or practice of "keeping Jesus in," how do we manage to do that away from church when we're at home, at work, at school, in the larger community?

And therein rests my point. The major failing of our contemporary faith witness is our accommodation of the secular in order not to offend. We do not throw out the ways of world and keep Jesus in by concentrating on God and the guidance offered in His Word; rather we have perfected the art of folding the world's ways into our faith. When we do that we are not separate, distinct and set apart as followers of Jesus are to be. Jesus is clear that we do not belong to the world, but to Him. (John 15:19) And because of that relationship, we cannot blend the secular perspective into the sacred as one does sugar into butter when making a pound cake. As followers of Jesus, we are commanded to teach the gospel and make disciples. We can't do that if we purposely leave Jesus out of our words, thoughts and deeds. That's what has us in the mess we're in today. The older lady had it right. In the name of Jesus there is no duality of religious practice, no duality of faith.

14

MASKED CHRISTIANITY

"Woe to you, teachers of the law and the Pharisees, you hypocrites! You are like whitewashed tombs, which look beautiful on the outside but on the inside are full of dead men's bones and everything unclean. In the same way, on the outside you appear to people as righteous but on the inside you are full of hypocrisy and wickedness."
                                              Matthew 23:27–29

As I reflected upon Jesus' "Seven Woes" sermon spoken in the temple court to the disciples and crowd gathered there, the opening lines of Paul Laurence Dunbar's poem "We Wear the Mask" came to mind. "We wear the mask that grins and lies. It hides our cheeks and shades our eyes." In many respects those to whom Jesus spoke wore masks too; masks of religiosity that hid who they really were; masks that covered their unrighteousness and hypocrisy. Unlike the people in Dunbar's poem who wore masks to hide their pain, subjugation and oppression in order to survive in a hostile environment, the scribes and religious leaders of that day hid the truth of who they were to maintain their status and power. And their actions of appearing to be who they were not were an obvious anathema to Jesus.

More than 2,000 years later, things haven't changed all that much. We modern day believers, Christians we call ourselves, too often mimic our ancestors to whom Jesus spoke. Easily we wear masks of religiosity that hide who we really are. These masks of "connection, purpose and insight" have become the symbols of our faith. And we have grown increasingly comfortable with their fit, convinced that we are all right with the Lord. To suggest otherwise is akin to throwing the gauntlet. After all, from the perspective of the mask wearer, being connected to the faith community is expected of the believer. Volunteer service gives purpose and reminds us that Christ came to serve, not to be served. And Bible study is necessary to further understanding of God's word. All things considered, it is hard to find fault with these understandings; until we consider them in the light of the "Woes" message. Like the whitewashed tomb, the masks of connection, purpose and insight give the outward appearance of cleanliness, of righteousness. From the vantage point of the whitewashed tomb or the mask all appears well. But when we apply Jesus' litmus test, we find who we say we are falls short of the mark.

The world sees the mask; God sees the heart. He sees into our motives in all these disciplines of faith. And He judges our righteousness not by what others see nor by the masks we wear. What difference does it make if we are connected to the church yet within that connection remain exclusive rather than inclusive; hearers only of the Word and not doers? What difference does it make if we offer service for the recognition it brings rather than humbly as the hands and feet of Christ? And what difference does it make if we study God's word during Bible study and fail to apply what we learn? These disciplines of the faith, these masks we present to the world, have one sole purpose—transforming us from the inside out to what and who God wants us to be.

If the teachers of the law and the Pharisees had been transformed by what they taught, their righteousness would have been evident to all. They would have understood that Jesus was the fulfillment of the law. When we understand in our faith journey that connection, service and biblical insight are the agents of transformation, God desires, there will be no need for masks. We will be who we proclaim as God's glory manifests itself in our lives. Jesus came to transform the world to be in right relationship with God the Father. Mask wearers don't get that. They continue to hide the truth of who they are. Jesus' "Woe" sermon is as relevant today for them as it was to those who heard His words in the temple courts.

15

Powerful Weakness

"My grace is sufficient for you, for my power is made perfect in weakness."

2 Corinthians 12:9

Powerful weakness—an oxymoron for certain. If we don't get anything else, we get that power's very definition is an antonym for the word weakness. And for sure in this 21st century there is no power in weakness, just the opposite. So it's not surprising when we read of that missionary extraordinaire, the Apostle Paul and his prayer that God would remove from him a "thorn in the flesh" (three times he pleaded that this weakness be taken away), we grasp that he understood the limits of weakness, irrespective of its guise.

God answered Paul's prayer, though perhaps not as Paul initially wished. As we read His response in the scripture above, we can't help but ponder, "What was God really saying to Paul?" And more importantly, what does that response say to us? Two possible answers come to mind as this disciple hurries to keep up with the one who continues to say, "Follow me." First, God wants us to understand that no matter what troubles us, be it physical handicaps, emotional challenges or spiritual poverty, His grace is sufficient in every circumstance. It is only by His grace that we live and have our being in the first place. We didn't will ourselves into existence. We do not sustain our lives by our own will. God's grace allows all this and in that allowance is the sufficiency. Secondly, God's power manifests itself when our power is revealed to be no power at all. Our culture equates power with strength. The stronger we are in health, in wealth, in possessions, and position, the more power we acquire and yield. When this is the case, God's power gets pushed aside or not even recognized as the ultimate power that makes the secular expressions of power possible. God knows that for us to really "get it", to really grasp His Omnipotence, we must often be stripped of the very things by which we define our power and sufficiency. It is in these weakened states of dependency that God is best able to manifest His greatness, power and sovereignty.

Two stories come to mind, one biblical and one in the here and now. Consider Job's story. He was stripped of everything—health, wealth, possessions, and offspring—before he finally accepted that power resides with and in God alone. But he didn't get that until he became the poster boy for secular weakness sustained by God's power. And in the here and now, that is the story of my cousin Ruth and her husband. Approximately twelve years ago, she was diagnosed with early stage Alzheimer disease. The ruthlessness of the disease has all but destroyed her physically and mentally, and of course taken its toll on her husband who has been until recently, her primary caregiver while still working. I see in his adjustment to this hand of fate over which he had no control a Pauline-like surrender. In their combined weakness battling this "thorn in the flesh," God has shown the power of His promise to not forsake them, but to walk with them through this life circumstance. It is God's power that is sufficient for them.

When we stand before Him totally dependent, in our states of imperfection, He brings His power to bear, to turn what seems impossible to possible; to take the broken vessel we are and reshape it to be what He intends. We are most pliable, most ready for that reshaping when our weakness is exposed and our only recourse is to turn to God. He alone knows what the best answer to our prayer is; most especially when our weakness spotlights His awesome power.

Paul says it best, *"Therefore I will boast all the more gladly about my weaknesses, so that Christ's power may rest on me... For when I am weak, then I am strong."* (2 Corinthians 12:9–10) Powerful weakness: an oxymoron from the secular perspective; a truth from the sacred.

16

Headed Where?

Jesus took the twelve aside and told them, "We are going up to Jerusalem, and everything that is written by the prophets about the Son of Man will be fulfilled."...After Jesus said this, he went on ahead, going up to Jerusalem.

Luke 18:33; 19:28

Scripture tells us that Jesus, as His earthly ministry drew to a close, set His face toward Jerusalem; and without hesitation He walked steadfastly toward it. As those who embrace the Christian faith, we might wisely ask ourselves, "Where are we headed? What or where is our Jerusalem? Key questions for the 21st century disciple. On a literal level, Jesus was headed to a specific geographical location: the city of Jerusalem; but his journey to that place represented so much more than just a final destination. Jerusalem would be the culminating event that would change the world because it was the fulfillment of God's purpose for His life—crucifixion on a cross and resurrection from a tomb.

I suspect few of us when we cast our lot with the Savior think of that decision in light of the journey upon which we are embarking. And I'd wager even fewer ponder "What is my Jerusalem? As Jesus' words indicate, He understood his ending well before He began His beginning. I don't think we can just say, "Oh, well, that's to be expected. He was God's Son after all." But Jesus' humanity enabled Him to experience life as we live it. And because He did, it means we have the capacity once we accept Him as Lord and Savior to do the same. We can respond to the questions. Now some might say their "Jerusalem" is simply learning to live on earth as good Christians, to arrive at a place of peace and joy and brotherhood in their communities, nation and world. Others will proclaim their "Jerusalem" is Heaven, the final station where the faithful disembark.

In my understanding (and I admit I'm still a work in progress), our Jerusalem is a combination of both the destination and the journey to get there. In many ways the destination is the easier of the two to grasp. We understand "end times": the culmination of God's interaction with His creation on earth as we know it. His son, our Lord and Savior Jesus the Christ, will return in final victory over Satan and sin. Yes, we get the destination aspect of our Jerusalem. It's the journey toward it that causes pause. Living in the here and now, being in the world but not of the world are aspects of the journey we find harder to navigate. Setting our face toward Jerusalem forces choices: short-cuts versus the long routes; long term versus short term benefits; doing church versus being the church; the path less traveled versus the more popular wider lanes. Ask anyone who knows me relatively well what my favorite thing to do is and my favorite season and they'll likely respond without much hesitation: shopping and Christmas. Over the years this pastime and season always put extra pep in my step. And as you might imagine I have paid the price (and in all honesty still pay the price) for my overindulgence in both. When engaged in either, the furthest thing from mind is my journey to "Jerusalem." At least that has been the case for most of my adult Christian life. It is only in more recent years that I have begun to reconcile my desires and my "Jerusalem" journey. Clearly the choice is mine; the road to Jerusalem is the narrow road, the one on which the disciple shops mostly for needs and not wants; the road upon which the disciple marks the celebration of Jesus' birth with worship, not extravagant gift buying. I am making progress. Last year for the first time since I can remember during my annual visit, my baby sister and I did not make the customary drive to our favorite outlet mall to buy handbags, shoes, and other items we typically do not need.

A familiar story is told in the Gospel of Luke of the rich man who accumulated more than he would ever need. Jesus declared him a "fool." He didn't realize that all he had would amount to nothing once he was gone; that others would get what he had spent his resources on. It's no different for today's disciple whose face is set toward "Jerusalem." Choosing the narrow road eliminates distractions; limits the baggage to just the essential carry-on; requires focus to avoid missteps and twisted ankles; allows room for God's Spirit to dictate the direction.

17

Jesus Rest

Come to me, all you who are weary and burdened, and I will give you rest.

Matthew 11:28

Such a sweeping, inclusive invitation Jesus offers to everyone regardless of status or stature. Notice that there are no strings attached to the invite; no gift registry card or mention of required attire is included. The only requirement seems to be that of the human condition. And it resonates; for who isn't at some point weary of life's unending demands, trials and tribulations, challenges borne upon sagging shoulders? Scripture informs us that Jesus was in the town of Galilee preaching and teaching when He spoke these words. He could just as easily be in a pulpit, a convention arena, a television studio or on a street corner and the words would still ring true for us today. In this 21st century despite societal advances that would boggle the mind of our biblical ancestors, we live shackled both by burdens similar to theirs and others more specific to our time. Many battle financial insufficiencies traceable to various causes: unemployment and under employment leading the list. Increasing numbers battle diseases and declining health. Family dynamics shift and what was once a sure foundation for children and young people fragments, dysfunctional families become more the norm. Greed drives the market place; politics thrives on conflict and dishonesty; public service betrays the trust of the very people who depend upon it; and the "isms"—racism, classism, and sexism—spiral.

We ask in our weariness, "Is there any relief?" Surely this is not the abundant life the Scriptures promise. What are we to do? This disciple suggests we begin by recalling words of the iconic hymn, *Lift Every Voice and Sing*. "God of our weary years, God of our silent tears, thou who hast brought us thus far on the way, Thou who hast by Thy might, led us into the light, keep us forever in the path we pray. Lest our feet stray from the places, our God where we met Thee; lest our hearts, drunk with the wine of the world, we forget Thee. Shadowed beneath Thy hand, may we forever stand, true to our God…" These lyrics remind us that even in the midst of our weariness, our trials, our tears, God has not forsaken us; in fact He has kept His hand upon us and guided our steps even when we have strayed. Jesus' invitation is but a reminder that the source of our rest, our respite in times of weariness is readily available. Within His sacred Word are the gems of relief we crave; somewhat like what we experience when we dissolve the Alka Seltzer tablet in water and drink it to relieve our indigestion. Irrespective of its source, when we ingest God's Word during times of weariness, it brings the relief Jesus offers in this invitation.

I recall perhaps that most dreaded weariness producer: the death of a loved one and that moment when you gather for the internment rites at the cemetery. As I waited to depart the burial site of my husband, the hole in my heart throbbing, my oldest brother whispered to me, "Bev, read the Book of Job, one chapter a day." He didn't elaborate. I began the next day to do just that. Along with other devotional materials, I reread Job. Though I was no stranger to the story, the words came alive as they never had before. In these scriptures was just the "rest" I needed to begin the navigation of my new world, to relieve the sorrow that engulfed me. Those forty days of nourishing "rest" lifted my weariness. Perhaps now is the time, dear reader, for you to discover that same relief. Hopefully you haven't thrown away the Savior's invite; maybe just tossed it aside into that box reserved for the things you'll get to one day. Behold! That day has arrived. Jesus' divine invitation is the only relief available for what ails you. Some will say, "Toss off your weariness and your burdens and go to Him." I say, "Forget that!" The invitation is wide open; take your heartache and pain and sorrow, your weariness with you and Go! He's extended the invitation. He awaits your response. My youngest grandson had a saying he proclaimed when he was about to begin some six year old adventure. Joyfully, he would say, "Let's get this party started!" It's that spirit of anticipation we need to bring to Jesus' invitation. Open your Bibles and let's get this Holy Ghost weariness-eliminator party started!

18

What Do You Want Me To Give You?

That night God appeared to Solomon and said to him, "Ask for whatever you want me to give you."

2 Chronicles 1:7

What a mind boggling question! Can you even imagine it? Solomon has inherited the kingship from his father King David, and as he begins to consolidate his position, God poses this question. And perhaps just as startling is Solomon's response: *"You have shown great kindness to David my father and have made me king in his place… Give me wisdom and knowledge, that I may lead this people…"* It's kind of hard to imagine that was his answer to the divine question. Most folk I know would probably have said, "Lord, give me wealth, success, victory over my haters, happiness, long life," or any number of other material blessings. But not Solomon; just give me "wisdom and knowledge." His answer pleased God and because of it, God gave him not only what he asked for, but as verse twelve reads, *"… And I will also give you wealth, riches and honor, such as no king who was before you ever had none after you will have."* Wow!

And over the greater part of his rule as king, Solomon was renowned for his wise counsel, great riches and devotion to God. When he finished building God's temple as instructed, God spoke to him again and renewed His covenant that He had made earlier. If Solomon continued to obey and observe God's decrees and laws there would always be a Davidic descendant upon the throne. But God also warned Solomon of the consequences should he turn away and forsake those laws and decrees and worship other gods. (Alas, those pesky consequences just stand in the wings, waiting).

This brings me to the point of this reflection. Solomon, full of wisdom and knowledge, understanding God's laws and decrees, blessed beyond comprehension with every material thing he could desire, forfeits it all in the final years of his reign by turning aside to idols and pagan worship. What caused this downfall from God's grace? Fast forward several millennia. His downfall was caused by the same thing that causes us today to live outside God's commandments and purposes: disobedience. We ignore God's word and in so doing forget that all we have both intellectually and materially comes from Him. We discover as did Solomon that our intellect will not save us; neither will our fame and fortune.

Like our biblical ancestor, we have short memories. We come to believe our own press; that we are responsible for the grace and favor we enjoy. We slide into idol worship without great fanfare. Solomon succumbed to the influence of foreign wives (who he shouldn't have married in the first place) who brought their gods with them to the marriage bed. We too slip easily into practices and behaviors that transgress our faith. One "little" sin follows another and before long, we have forsaken the disciplines of discipleship to embrace the idols of the secular culture of the day.

The good news for us is as it was for Solomon, to whom God was still merciful even after his disobedience. (2 Kings 11:9–13) By Jesus' atonement on the cross for our sins, God's mercy covers a multitude of our sins. We are pardoned by Jesus' shed blood and His resurrection from death. His sacrifice for us allows reconciliation with God Himself. Because of His grace and mercy, we must strive daily to resist the idols that dot the landscape of our journey, obeying instead the Master's call for obedience to His teachings.

19

Packing Pastors

For though we live in the world, we do not wage war as the world does. The weapons we fight with are not the weapons of the world.

2 Corinthians 10:4

The headline of the article caught my attention—"Piece be with you: Pastors pack heat." According to the article, some pastors in the Detroit, Michigan area have taken to carrying guns as a strategy to combat rising violence. One of the pastors justified this rather unorthodox practice by explaining that as a pastor, he has a responsibility as the shepherd to watch over his flock. And that reasoning is the rationale for the "piece," i.e. gun, in the pulpit; it's a way to protect the church's parishioners. It is my opinion that this thinking doesn't align with what the Bible teaches.

Millenniums before Mahatma Gandhi and Martin Luther King Jr. espoused the philosophy and practice of nonviolence, Jesus personified and lived it. He taught: *"Do not resist an evil person. If someone strikes you on the right cheek, turn to him the other also."* (Matthew 5:39) Our faith as Christians requires that we live in the world without allowing the world and its values and mores to live in us. We cannot, as one of the pastors suggests, adjust to society. The one pastor's assertion that it's okay to supplement our faith with weapons and "to use our God-given talents to protect ourselves" flies in the face of the gospel's message as noted above in 2 Corinthians. How is our faith in evidence if we so easily adopt the world's ways when we are confronted by evil? To reach the conclusion that the only way to protect ourselves is to take up arms against the criminal element in our midst suggests that faith in God's omnipotence and in Jesus Christ our Savior has sadly eroded. And for the clergy to make this claim is even sadder.

Romans 8:28 tells us that nothing can separate us from the love of God in Christ Jesus. In my mind that includes violence and criminal activity. It is difficult to imagine Jesus shooting a thief; it is easier to see Him instead offer whatever else was not already taken. I realize many will take issue with this position and say this kind of thinking is no longer germane to the times in which we live. I disagree. If we are who we claim to be, i.e. followers and disciples of Jesus, we live daily with an unshakable faith that God is in control; even when danger threatens and our mortal lives are on the line. As Christians we understand the faith journey has its peaks and its valleys; that we are not immune to challenges and difficulties; that our faith will be tested. Like the Hebrew boys threatened with death who declared that God was able to save them from the fiery furnace, but even if He did not, they would not worship any other gods nor bow to any golden image (Daniel 3:16–18), we cast our lot with Christ; assured that whether we live or die, we are on the Lord's battlefield. Our victory is already won.

So perhaps our pastors are well advised to reconsider their stance. Maybe rather than packing guns, they should consider the examples of the apostles who were charged with preaching the good news of Jesus Christ. They did so under peril of assault and even death. Yet the Bible records not one of them arming themselves with weapons when they spoke to the crowds or in the synagogues. And well they might have as they were often under attack from opponents and skeptics. These "shepherds" followed Jesus' example of combating evil without resorting to the sword. Recall how He responded at the time of His betrayal in the garden when one of His followers cut off the ear of the solider about to arrest Him. He didn't resist arrest or act violently. No, He admonished His follower—*"No more of this," and then touched the man's ear and healed him.* (Luke 22:51) Jesus was not a warrior Savior; He expects those He calls to shepherd believers to model His actions. A pastor packing a "piece"/weapon in the pulpit is doing just the opposite.

20

Prodigal Son

But while he was still a long way off, his father saw him and was filled with compassion for him… the father said, "This son of mine was dead and is alive again; he was lost and is found."
Luke 15:20, 24

What's guaranteed to send a believer, especially a "seasoned saint" scrambling to her Bible? A sudden, reason- defying tragedy allowed by God. And typically the scripture search is targeted to the words that offer comfort and hope for a particular situation. I confess I'm no exception, though I lay no claim to sainthood. On January 27, 2016 when my son was admitted to the neuro ICU of Emory University Hospital following an emergency room visit, I plunged into familiar passages in the New Testament. Over the next weeks as his condition spiraled downward, I drew upon the many biblical accounts of Jesus healing the sick, the afflicted, the troubled for comfort and reassurance. The Gospels recount how Jesus rebuked the fever of Simon's mother-in-law and it left her; His touch upon the man with leprosy and he was immediately cleansed of the disease; His reward for the faithful friends who interceded for their paralytic companion by cutting a hole in the roof to lower him so Jesus could say, *"Get up. Take your mat and go home;"* His healing from afar the servant of the centurion who in faith believed if Jesus would *"But say the word, and my servant will be healed;"* the widow's son who was thought dead to whom

He said, *"Young man, I say to you, get up."* And he sat up and began to talk; His healing of the man possessed by demons; the woman with the long term bleeding disorder whom He healed because of her faith that if she could just touch the hem of His garment, she would be cured; His instruction to Jairus, the synagogue ruler, when someone told him his daughter was dead—*"Don't be afraid. Just believe, and she will be healed."* And Jesus took her by the hand and said simply, *"My child, get up,"* and she did; His healing of the boy with the evil spirit whom the disciples were unable to heal; the crippled woman to whom Jesus spoke, *"Woman, you are set free from your infirmity"* and immediately she straightened up; His healing of the ten lepers; His words to the blind beggar, *"Receive your sight. Your faith has healed you;"* His restoration of mobility to the lame man who had lain by the pool in Bethesda for 38 years; His restoration of sight to the man who was born blind; His healing of the deaf and mute man brought to Him by the villagers. *"...the people brought to Jesus all who had various kinds of sickness, and laying his hands on each one, he healed them."* (Luke 4:40)

These accounts testify to the healing power Jesus offers to those who believe He can heal; they inform my faith foundation and assure me that what He did for others then, He continues to do for us now. And so it is with this faith that my son will be healed and restored that I compare our story to that of the parable of the prodigal son. We often think the son was solely responsible for his downward spiral and perhaps in large measure he was. But what dynamics played into his ill-advised choices are unknown. All we have is the story of a young man who had everything and lost it all. His descent into poverty and being able to only find work at the local pigsty speak to the devastating conditions of his life. And though my son's path does not mirror the prodigal, nonetheless he finds himself presently in similar circumstances: a place of devastation. And because we don't know where the conscious mind goes when it appears dormant, we don't know his thoughts at this point. But what I do know is I am much like the father in one very important way. Just think, for that father to see his son approaching from afar that day means he was on the lookout for him every day. He kept his eyes peered toward the direction from which he would appear; that kind of vigilance required faith. He woke up every morning anticipating his son's return; he searched the horizon for that familiar gait. He even kept the best robe hanging in the closet with the best pair of sandals underneath and a fattened calf in the freezer. He knew the day would come. His son who was lost would return home!

And I'm like that dad. I awaken each day filled with the hope that this will be the day the son of my heart returns from his time with the Lord. I am confident that as I sit by his bedside watching, talking to him, reading scripture and words of encouragement that his sojourn in the netherworld of brain injury will end; my faith gives me the resolve to approach each moment as if it will be the moment of revival! Quentin will "come to his senses" (Luke 15); as the prodigal son was healed of his waywardness and rebellion, God will heal Quentin of all that presently afflicts him. The day is coming when he will be welcomed in love and restored to his place in the arms of all who love him. He'll sport that new Polo shirt and those Edmond Allen lace ups. Somebody will fire up the grill and the celebration will begin! A faithful mom never stops looking, hoping and believing her son who is "lost" will be "found."

21

Jehovah Jireh

"And my God will meet all your needs according to his glorious riches in Christ Jesus."

Philippians 4:19

Paul wrote these words millennia ago and they are as true now as then. God continues to meet our needs as our provider, our "Jehovah Jireh." This aspect of God's character manifests in the ordinary and the extraordinary facets of our lives. A few days ago, a stranger entered my son's hospital room where he is being treated for a hemorrhagic brain induced stroke. The gentleman introduced himself as Bill, a seventy one year old stroke survivor who volunteers in the Brain Injury Peer Support Program. With little prompting, he shared his story; a chronicle I believe illustrates the scripture above and makes us say, "Look at God!"

Bill and his wife were up late that particular night at their cabin in the north Georgia Mountains watching a movie. Before going to bed, he took the smaller of their two dogs out to do doggy business. It was his custom, he recalled, to always close the door behind him when he left the house. But that night for some reason he left it slightly ajar. Flashlight in hand, he and the dog set off. Without any warning after he'd walked some ways from the cabin, his flashlight fell out of his hand and when he bent to pick it up, his hand would not close around it. Though he realized something was wrong, his first concern was for the small dog that scampered ahead of him into the darkness. Too far away from the house to call for his wife, he shouted for the dog instead. "Go get momma," he told the dog when it reappeared. "Go get momma." Because Bill had not completely shut the door, the small dog was able to nose its way into the house; immediately it began barking. It alerted the larger dog that joined in and the combined ruckus drew Bill's wife from the bedroom to see what was going on. Concerned that the dog was home without Bill, she ventured outside, calling his name. Guided by the fallen flashlight that lay on the ground, she found Bill, now unable to get up on his own. After getting him back to the cabin and giving him two aspirins, (as she suspected a stroke) she called 911.

Time was of the essence as the paramedics prepared to transport Bill to the local hospital. One or perhaps it was both of the EMTs remembered that Emory Hospital had recently opened a unit at another hospital in the remote mountain area that specialized in treating stroke victims. They took him there. Bill concluded his story with the comment, "Things just seemed to fall into place for me. Had I not left the door cracked, the dog wouldn't have gotten in and I might have lain there a while before my wife realized I hadn't come to bed. If the flashlight had broken when I dropped it, she wouldn't have known where to begin looking for me because it was so dark outside. And if the EMT personnel had not known about the Emory stroke unit at that particular hospital, I would not have received the immediate attention stroke victims need at the local community hospital and probably not have survived"

Now Bill's "Everything fell into place" comment may be true. But to the believer and follower of Jesus Christ, his story demonstrates much more. Bill's experience is a classic example of Jehovah Jireh doing what He does best: providing for our needs in ways that on the surface appear ordinary. Each event in this amazing chronicle shouts, "God provides." A door always closed, but that night left ajar; A flashlight whose light bulb doesn't break when it hits the ground; A small dog who heeds his master's call to go for help; A light that guides a wife to her fallen husband; Emergency transport personnel who remember a better alternative; An affiliation between a small rural hospital and a major urban hospital renowned for its treatment of brain injuries; so much more than "falling into place." This story speaks to "divine appointments;" God orchestrations that give life to the words penned by the Apostle Paul for the church at Philippi. God meets our needs. He is our provider. Bill's story is especially inspiring to anyone to whom life's trials spring unanticipated and unannounced. It illustrates that before the trial begins, during its duration and after it ends, God is in the provision business, meeting our "needs according to his glorious riches."

22

Testing Time Testimony

"Naked I came from my mother's womb, and naked I will depart. The Lord gave and the Lord has taken away; may the name of the Lord be praised... Shall we accept good from God, and not trouble?" In all this Job did not sin in what he said.

Job 1:21; Job 2:10

I'm not suggesting my story in anyway is the equivalent of Job's. But I can see similarities as I sit here in the ICU room where my son lies prostrate in an unconscious state, right side unmoving and respiratory functions supported by a ventilator; this state caused by an acute hemorrhage in his left brain. I cannot claim Job's righteousness as described in the Old Testament. But I can say I am a committed follower of Jesus Christ who strives daily to live out the call to discipleship by following His example. What Job and I do have in common is the experience of "testing time." Job was a good man, living his life in a manner that glorified God. But despite his regular expressions of devotion and piety, his religiosity, disaster struck. Without warning God allowed him to lose all he had materially and personally. In several swoops of devastation, wealth, health and family were taken. Only his wife survived, but her lack of faith in God was just another burden Job had to bear. Such was Job's devastation, even his friends proved to be of no support as they thought surely he must have done something wrong for God to visit this desolation upon him.

Testing Time Testimony

Whereas Job's testing time appears to have occurred over the course of several days, my time frame is divided into two distinct segments. Eight years ago, I lived and worshipped God in a manner I felt was Christ like; daily I worked on a book of devotionals I felt He had led me to write. My husband and I attended church regularly; I taught Bible study classes and worked on a women's prayer line. Like Job I had no warning that testing time was upon me. One Sunday evening as we relaxed in front of the television, it struck. My husband went from smiling and conversation to seizures and what in an hour or so would be diagnosed cardiac arrest, most likely from a blood clot to the heart. Like a lightning strike, life as I had known it for almost thirty five years flashed and was gone. And now eight years later, the devastator has struck again. My son's complaint of lightheadedness, some imbalance and a headache culminated into his being struck down by a major stroke. At the time of his affliction, we lived together – he, my daughter in law and three of my four grandchildren; acclimated to multi-generational living in a home comfortable enough to accommodate us all.

Testing time for me has been as it was for Job a defining moment of faith. And while I have no one in my circle of friends who would dare say, "Curse God and die," I have had to combat my own fears and anxieties. Somewhat like Job, I have wrestled with the questions that unexpected, unexplained tragedies bring. And while he could only speak his queries aloud, I have turned as we are prone to do in this day and age to the internet and Google for my answers. And as I did eight years ago, I have wondered though not voiced, "Why my son? Am I not living my life as your servant in such a manner that you would spare him this devastation? Do I not lift him and his family up to you daily for protection and their wellbeing and prosperity?" Like Job I thought I was covering all my bases in my own spiritual disciplines for myself and my family. But what I've had to accept as I had to accept eleven years ago is God is in control of His world and all He created to live in it. He made my husband; he made my son. They belong first and foremost to Him and have been and are on loan to me. My understanding of God's purposes is limited to my minuscule mind and its limitations. Even now as I sit bedside wanting to do something, anything to ease his condition, watching the health care professionals attend him, I accept I cannot. Only God can heal his body and restore him to wellness and wholeness. So like Job, I am forced to say, "I know that you alone can do all things; no plan of yours can be thwarted…" And in the parlance of contemporary expression, I acknowledge that God is omnipotent, omniscient and omnipresent. He knows what He is doing with this son of my heart. He is in control of his healing and knows what needs to be done before it crosses the minds of his earthly physicians. He is here in the room with us, His Spirit hovering, nudging, guiding, comforting. Yes, it's faith testing time. Do I trust Him with this gift of life He gave me? Yes, I do. His best for my son will be more than I can think or imagine. And we sing His praises even before we see the manifestation of His handiwork.

23

Letting Go

"Forget the former things and do not dwell on the past. See, I am doing a new thing. Now it springs up; do you not perceive it?"
Isaiah 43:18–19

Nostalgia for the past is nothing new, as these words of the Lord to the prophet Isaiah attest. As far back in recorded time as the Babylonian era, people have sought solace in their memories of the way things used to be. But the Lord challenges us to let go of what was and instead embrace what He is doing now. He was intentional in these words to the Israelites who were at that moment still in captivity; in all probability they didn't understand. All they remembered was how great it was "back in the day." What they failed to grasp and what we likewise fail to understand is that we cannot truly serve God and His purposes until we have completely surrendered, "let go," of self to Him. And that means most often letting go of the past.

But God loves us and knows how difficult it is for us to do that. Consider Jesus' word to the young man who falls on his knees and asks, *"Good teacher, what must I do to inherit eternal life?"* (Mark 10:21–22) The Bible reads that Jesus *"looked at him and loved him."* And then proceeded to say, *"Go, sell everything you have and give to the poor, and you will have treasure in heaven. Then come, follow me."* And we know the young man's reaction; his face fell and he went away sad because he was very wealthy. Jesus was asking him to forget his past, what he had acquired, what he owned, and his status in the community and instead embrace the new thing Jesus was doing in that time and place.

We are not too different than that young man. For many reasons we cling to what was, afraid to venture beyond the known and familiar. The young man in all his earnestness could not envision life without his wealth and life style. In our time we elect to stay in the "toddler stages" of our faith. We've mastered church fellowship, reading the scriptures and "kinda sorta" praying. What we do, we do our way. "I'll do that Lord; just as soon as I do this." "But Lord, we've always done it this way and frankly I don't see any reason to change things. I know You are God and everything, but tradition does have its place." As He did for the young man He does now for us. He says that in order to follow Him, we must abandon our all for Him, not as we will, but as He wills for us. In our acceptance of His forgiveness, salvation and grace, we understand we no longer lead the parade. He is the Drum Major and we yield our baton to Him and the new thing He is doing.

And that new thing may very well require we give up things we've worked hard to acquire or achieve. That's as difficult for some to contemplate as it was for the young man. We may give some, but all? To follow Jesus? How is that possible in today's world? If we give up everything, will we not become just like those to whom we're asked to give? Jesus' words were and are a stumbling block. And this stumbling block takes us back to the Isaiah scripture. As disciples of Jesus Christ, we recognize that clinging to the spoils of the world will not lead us to eternal life. We understand God is moving today toward His promises of tomorrow; and for those who believe and trust in Him, the "new thing" He expects His followers to perceive is the behaviors and attitudes that lead to eternal life. Living in the past and resting in the present do nothing except maintain the status quo; and we do not serve a "status quo" God. In our homes, in our churches, in our communities, God seeks to do a new thing in and through us. He calls us in each

Letting Go

of these environments to surrender everything that opposes His purposes and plans. He calls us who are known by His name to be witnesses that "letting go" is letting God be God.

24

EFFECTIVE PRAYER

The prayer of a righteous man is powerful and effective.

James 5:16

Within the recent three months, I have witnessed prayers for those with life threatening diseases being answered and denied. In one instance, despite daily fervent prayers being offered for her healing, a dear friend succumbed to a six month battle with cancer; in the other, as the same intensity of fervent prayer was offered, my youngest brother was spared when a donor was found for his double organ transplant just as a decision was rendered to remove his name from the list because he was too ill for the procedure to be effective. In both cases, those who prayed were faithful followers of Jesus and believed in the power of prayer. Why does God answer prayers for healing for some and not for others? It's a question the faithful typically don't dwell upon because it seems to question God's omnipotence. After all, He is God all by Himself and He does what He chooses according to His will and purposes. And perhaps therein is our answer.

Oswald Chambers writes, "But remember that we have to ask of God things that are in keeping with the God whom Jesus Christ revealed." For me that prompts the question, "Exactly what did Jesus reveal about His Father, our God?" What do we know of Him through Scripture that guides our requests as we pray? And after we pray, helps us accept His "Yes" or "No." Perhaps the first thing we are to understand is that we do not pray with a "Wish List" of things, provisions or positions. The Gospel of Luke reads that God knows our secular needs and will make provision for them. We are told to *"seek first his kingdom and these things will be given to you as well."* (Luke 12:30–31)

From the teachings of the Savior comes the answer: the seeking of God's kingdom. In other words as Chambers states, we pray asking God for those things which insure we are on one accord with Him. There is no clearer picture of what it means to seek God's kingdom than the teachings Jesus spoke in the Beatitudes. (Matthew 5–7) In them Jesus reveals God's expectations for our godly living, His laws and commandments, and His promises to the faithful. In both the Old and New Testaments, the characteristics of God with which we are to be aligned point to His omnipotence; to the fact that His thoughts are not our thoughts, neither are our ways his ways; that He has purposes that exceed our understanding. (Isaiah 55:8–11)

As we lay our petitions before God, when we are on one accord with Him, we acknowledge His divinity and His Sovereignty. We humbly surrender our will to His higher will and purpose, both for ourselves and for those for whom we pray. We pray for greater faith and hope, believing that He will supply what we need when we need it. We recall that He has a plan for everyone whose creation He has allowed. We further admit that what we see in the natural is nothing like what He sees, so we ask for wisdom and discernment. And because we trust His plans are far superior to ours, we ask that His best plan will be forthcoming, no matter what that might be; even if that plan is not at all that for which we pray. So we pray for patience as we await His answer. We understand that His timing does not run on the same clock as ours. Scripture reminds us, *"For a thousand years in your sight are like a day that has just gone by, or like a watch in the night."* (Psalm 90:4) And finally, we come to grips with the seeming arbitrariness of answered prayer by recalling Job's belated understanding of who this God is. Can the clay make demands of the potter? Or question his design? (Romans 9:20–21) From whose perspective does the world and all within have meaning? Only the Creator's. Being on one accord with God means we make our requests and leave the outcomes to His greater knowledge, wisdom and ultimate plans. Like Job, in humility we say, *"Surely I spoke of things I did not understand, things too wonderful for me to know…"* (Job 42:3)

25

Nothing is Impossible for God

"I tell you the truth; if you have faith as small as a mustard seed, you can say to this mountain, 'Move from here to there' and it will move."

Matthew 17:20–21

Something happened to me while I was in Dallas that I choose to call a miracle of faith. In fact it so stretches the imagination I was drawn to the 17th chapter of Matthew in coming to terms with it. The disciples had been unable to heal a young boy who was demon possessed and when they came to Jesus and asked why they had been unsuccessful, Jesus responded with the words above. Now I'll admit that in years past, I struggled with this scripture. The actuality of speaking a word and causing a mountain to move from one place to another defied rational thought. Probably like most Christians, I decided that Jesus was not being literal. The mountain was symbolic of the challenges and obstacles we face in life; by faith we move them from positions that impede our faith journey. That was my sense of that scripture until my devotional books went missing.

As I always do, I travel with my Bible and three or four devotional resources: the *Upper Room*, *Our Daily Bread*, and *My Utmost for His Highest*, etc. The morning I checked out of the hotel following my high school reunion, I remembered (or so I thought) placing them in the front pocket of my suitcase. Later that evening at my sister's home, when I looked for them, they were not there. I searched both inside and outside the luggage; as I ran my hand to the bottom of the front pocket for the umpteenth time, my sister who was watching me remarked, "They're not in there. It's empty. I can see your hand at the bottom and there's nothing there. You must have left them on the table in the hotel room." Frustrated, I stopped searching and called the hotel. Lost and Found was closed; I'd have to call back the next day. I sat on the bed and talked to the Lord. "You know how important those books are to me, Lord. What will I do in the morning? I can't start my day without my devotionals. I have my Bible, but I need my books. One of them as you know has notations from 2008! Lord, I know You know where my books are and I trust You to get them back to me tomorrow." At bedtime I reiterated my prayer and slept without further worry.

The next morning, the front desk told me the room had not yet been cleaned and they would have someone look for the books. My sister and I were poised to go retrieve them when something led me to look one more time. When I ran my hand into the very same front pocket I had searched so diligently the night before, I felt something. My books!

I ran to the stairs and shouted down, "I have my books! They were in the pocket I was searching last night." "Praise the Lord," my sister responded. "God is good. It's a miracle," I said. "How can this be?" "Don't question it; just accept it," my wise baby sister answered. And so I did; I accepted it as just that—a miracle. I never doubted that God would reunite me with my devotional resources. Since my room had not been cleaned, I assumed it would be a simple matter of the hotel calling to say they found them. That would have been answered prayer in the ordinary. But we serve a God who sometimes chooses to act extraordinarily on our behalf. And this was one of those times. He not only answered my prayers, but He did it so boldly. My books were just another mountain that needed moving "from here to there." He "moved" them from wherever they were the night before to where they were supposed to be.

I don't care what anyone else offers as an explanation for what occurred. "They were there all along. You just overlooked them. You thought you searched that pocket." I know what I know. The books were missing and then they were not. I believed God would restore them and He did. When we come to Him in faith, He is faithful; because for Him, nothing is impossible.

26

Parallels

Some of you may not see it, but the juxtaposition of Paul's situation as he relates it in his letter from prison to the church at Philippi to that of my son's hospitalization since January, 2016 is clear as crystal to me. I have read the passage in Philippians 1:12–26 on many occasions and studied it in some depth in Bible study sessions. But it was not until a few days ago when I read it as the background scripture for a devotional that the parallel of the apostle and Quentin resonated.

If you remember the passage, Paul writes to reassure the faithful in Philippi that though his imprisonment is difficult, they need to understand it from his perspective. Far from silencing him or muting the word he preached, his current situation has had the opposite impact. Because of it, the gospel was being advanced; his very confinement had given rise to the message of Jesus infiltrating his captors and others beyond the prison walls. And even more astonishing, his followers and believers were themselves emboldened and encouraged to speak God's word with courage and fearlessness. Paul goes on to proclaim that through the prayers offered up for him and the power of the Holy Spirit he will be delivered and continue to live. And yet he admits he is conflicted in his current state. For he clearly understands that if he were to die, his desire to be with Christ Jesus would be fulfilled; but at the same time he realizes that continued life will mean more fruitful labor on his part for the advancing of the gospel. And so he concludes that it is better at this time for him to "remain in the body" and continue the work to which he has been appointed, for the glory of God.

When I read this scripture to Quentin as part of our devotional time, I pointed out to him the parallels I saw. Like Paul in chains, confined to prison, he is in bondage too; not physical chains, but the chains of a disease that has confined him to a hospital bed unable to move of his own accord. And like Paul's situation, his hospitalization is difficult for him and for his family. Yet as the days have become weeks and weeks become months, this perspective of Paul's seems to define Quentin's trial. Because of his incapacitation, our faith as a family has mushroomed beyond anything we could ever imagine. That faith has opened our mouths to declare boldly and without hesitation that God is faithful and trustworthy and merciful and gracious; that His word is truth and He never fails to deliver on His promises.

Quentin's confinement in this disease prison has released prayer near and far on his behalf; it has sparked shared electronic devotionals, social media praise and prayer, testimonies to God's goodness and deliverance. He has become a symbol, if you will, of the modern day Job, afflicted seemingly without known cause of something that causes even the neurologists to shake their heads in puzzlement and wonder. Their expressions reveal their thoughts, "Why is he still alive?" Paul's realizes that he must continue the work; that it is not something done from the grave. I think this is one of the factors contributing to Quentin still being with us. In his subconscious I believe he understands that the work God has appointed him is far from finished. As a husband and father and even an adult son, there is much yet to be accomplished. And who better to carry the message of God's word than someone who has been in bondage, broken the chains of debilitating disease, and has a personal testimony of the grace and mercy God offers. But the primary factor responsible for his awakening each morning is prayer. Scripture informs us that the prayer of the righteous is powerful and effective. (James 5:16). Quentin's hearing is unimpaired; cognitively he understands the prayers spoken on his behalf impact his situation. Just today I saw him struggle to speak to our former pastor as he began to pray. It was such an enormous effort on Quentin's part to say something that the pastor paused until the effort exhausted him. Like Paul, Quentin understands that prayer and the power of the Holy Spirit will bring about his deliverance. And like Paul, Quentin will continue to fight the good fight to God's glory. Wherein then is the lesson for us? In the midst of any situation that imprisons us, we remember God is using that situation for His greater good. And the prayers offered in support and encouragement during these seasons will produce in us the joy of sharing the truth of the gospel of Jesus Christ.

27

WHO WRITES THE MUSIC?

"For I know the plans I have for you," declares the Lord, "plans to prosper you and not to harm you, plans to give you hope and a future."

Jeremiah 29:11

God writes the composition of our lives, and though He gives us free will to choose the notes we play, ultimately the "piece" is His creation. A discordant note played loudly yesterday in the composition of my day; at least it "sounded" that way at the time. On the way to an out-patient surgical appointment in bumper to bumper traffic, I listened to my son's frustrated tirade. He blasted verbally every aspect of this decision; from my choice of a doctor on the north side rather than the south side of town where we reside, to the appointment time which required driving in early morning rush hour traffic. As his rant escalated, a dull pain formed on the side of my head near the eye which necessitated the surgical appointment. My spirit, initially at peace and confident that this procedure would transpire without incident, began a slow downward spiral. Disappointment and hurt feelings began pushing me into an emotional place unsuitable for the moment. Eventually with his verbal tantrum spent and my wordless response resonating inside the car, he apologized. He acknowledged his insensitivity; his real issue being his anxiety and concern for my wellbeing coupled with the frustration of driving in Atlanta traffic, something he hates.

As we parked and found our way to the ambulatory surgical center, a measure of peace returned. A quick and efficient check in suggested all was in place; with no apprehension or anxiety I settled comfortably upon the bed in the curtained cubicle enjoying the warm blankets the nurse placed over me. Expecting her return to take my vitals, I was surprised when the curtain parted and a woman entered, introduced herself and said quickly, "I'm sorry, Mrs. Clopton, but your surgery has been canceled. Dr. Olsen is out of the country." Discordant notes filled the small enclosure: my questions—her answers. The mute numbness cloud that arose on the ride to the hospital resurfaced. This time my son's frustration was directed at the hospital staff; how dare they do this to his mother! As we made our way out, my cell phone rang. A prayer partner/ sister-friend called, hoping to pray with me before I went into surgery. After listening to a brief summation of what had transpired, she said, "Bev, God stopped this surgery. You don't know why. You may never know why, but you do know God always knows best. We pray for His will and we accept that He knows what's best for us."

Her on time call and commentary, God orchestrated I'm sure, pushed away the cloud that hovered. She was right on point! And as my son was quick to add, that was part of what he had been trying to convey, traffic frustrations aside; he didn't feel in his spirit that this should be done. I'll give him the benefit of the doubt, but in this morning-after reflection, I do see the Divine Composer crafting the notes of my life to fit the "piece" He is currently directing: my retinal problem and its resolution.

The dictionary defines discordance as something out of harmony or agreement. In a musical composition, a discordant note is harsh or unpleasant. Yesterday's experience may at first seem to have been just that—a harsh, unpleasant, bewildering experience. But as one who believes God does compose and direct my life, this note seemingly discordant on the surface is in reality just another example of God's divine orchestration. He knew when the doctor's schedule was mismanaged and the mistake made that this would occur. His purpose is being served now as I wait to reschedule; He will direct the outcome of that decision. Our lives proceed as God allows and within our own decision making. And as the composition of that life plays, we return over and over to the truth of His word, aptly expressed by our brother Job. *"Then Job replied to the Lord: "I know that you can do all things; no plan of yours is thwarted… Surely I spoke of things I did not understand, things too wonderful for me to know… My ears had heard of you but now my eyes have seen you…"* (Job 42:1–5) Who does things like that? Only an omnipotent God who sees all and knows all and wants the best for His children, that's who. I am at peace. He writes my music.

28

First Response Syndrome

God is our refuge and strength, an ever present help in trouble. Therefore we will not fear, though the earth gives way and the mountains fall into the heart of the sea, though its waters roar and foam and the mountains quake with their surging.

Psalm 46

Oswald Chambers poses a question worth pondering when he writes, "Can I face whatever are my struggles or trials secure in the reality of Jesus or do the vicissitudes of daily living throw me into a panic?" In other words, are we able to face life and its inherent challenges with the confidence of the psalmist who recognizes God as an ever present help, even when the very foundations of his existence appear to be falling apart?

If we are honest many of us will admit that despite our assertion of faith in God, our default position is not on automatic pilot when sudden trouble arises or when trials linger indefinitely. Few are wired to instantly seek the God they profess, confident of His ultimate rescue. Rather our initial response is hesitancy, born of our tendency to try and handle things first ourselves. Self-sufficiency first seems ingrained. And when our feeble efforts fail, our next response often is one of panic or faulty decision making. Consider the familiar story of Abraham and Sarah as prime example of the "first response syndrome."

The book of Genesis relates the story of Abraham (initially called

First Response Syndrome

Abram) whom God called to leave his homeland and go with his wife to another place where God promised to make him through his descendants into a great nation; a nation that would bring blessings to all other nations to follow. Now the only apparent problem with the promise was the fact that both Sarah (initially named Sarai) and Abram not only had no children, but were well past the ages to conceive them. The scriptures do not speak to a rising panic in either of them but we can imagine that as the years became decades and Sarai remained barren, there was some consternation, especially on her part. It's not surprising that as these attempts to birth descendants continued to fail, Sarai would decide to remedy the situation herself via the first recorded surrogate pregnancy. *"... so she said to Abram, the Lord has kept me from having children. Go, sleep with my maidservant; perhaps I can build a family through her."* Abram agreed to what Sarai said. (Genesis 16:1–3) And we of faith know that outcome; the best intentions when not directed by God have a tendency to sprout undesired repercussions.

Apparently neither Sarai nor Abram were willing to trust God's promises over the long haul. They were not truly confident that God is able to do what He says He will do and that for Him nothing is impossible. Confidence in God's word and surety in His power to do what He promises are the major attributes of Faith. Unfortunately like our biblical ancestors, often we only embrace these attributes after our misguided attempts fail.

An important mark of Christian maturity is the realization that when crises erupt or problems continue unresolved, our first response always is to go to God, the author and finisher of our faith. Why would we even think of crafting our own solutions? Surely the God who said to Jeremiah, *"Before I formed you in the womb I knew you..."* knows each of us; and more importantly, knows both the beginning and end of our lives. As Christians we believe as David expresses in Psalm 139, *"When I was woven together in the depths of the earth, your eyes saw my unformed body. All the days ordained for me were written in your book before one of them came to be."* Strong faith formation acknowledges God's omnipotence. Believers whose quotients of confidence and surety are at maximum do not rely upon their own power, their own remedies or solutions. They understand the impossibility of trying to accomplish anything without God's guidance. They intentionally go first to God and there they wait, trusting that in His time and in His way, He will help them face the struggle or the crisis. They do not trust in their own understanding; they trust God in everything. They believe He will deliver on His promises.

29

Throwback Thursday

"From the Jews five times I received forty stripes minus one. Three times I was beaten with rods; once I was stoned; three times I was shipwrecked; a night and a day I have been in the deep; in journeys often, in perils of water, in perils of robbers, in perils of my own countrymen..."

2 Corinthians 11:24–27

One of the more recent phenomena of the social networking that has come to define a major element of modern society is something called "Throwback Thursday." Every Thursday individuals post memories of things that happened to them in the past on Facebook, Instagram, Twitter or other social networking sites. The postings provide a glimpse of who they were via photos or commentary.

Now I'm not knocking this latest craze, but it has made me consider this tentacle of social media from a theological perspective and ask, "Is there value in sharing our past in this way? And what might that value be?"

In the 2nd Corinthians scripture noted above, the Apostle Paul's epistle of incidents in his past are quite on par with the contemporary postings. Like today's Throwback Thursday poster, Paul is sharing who he was as evidenced by what happened to him in the past; a biblical "Throwback" writer. And while the contemporary postings seem to have little purpose other than recalling scenes of yesteryear in the lives of the posters, Paul's verbal photos suggest a higher one, at least to my way of thinking.

In this epistle to the church at Corinth, Paul lists the numerous hardships he has suffered over the years as an apostle of Jesus Christ. He makes it clear in this verbal "throwback" that serving God and living his life as a believer has not been easy. He drives home his point that despite his sufferings, he remains a true and committed apostle of the gospel. This original "Throwback" account sends a message to its hearers not only about Paul himself, but about the God they profess to serve. Looking back at what God had brought him through, Paul was able to point through these personal experiences to God's faithfulness and His demand that believers remain true to their faith. Quite similar to the writer of Psalm 78 who wrote of Israel's history to remind the people of God's faithfulness, Paul's throwback epistle reminds us how important it is to know our past as Christians and what being a disciple of Jesus Christ will require.

Few of us, if any, can compare our faith journey to the apostle's. Who among us can speak of shipwrecks, or prisons, of physical beatings or stoning? Not only did he suffer those atrocities for his faith, he also knew hunger and thirst; cold and nakedness; sleeplessness and weariness. In recalling those experiences and sharing those memories Paul speaks to the faithful these millenniums later. These "throwback" accounts bring to mind our personal walk with the Lord. When God has been faithful and delivered us from trials or suffering, sometimes for our beliefs, but more often as part of the human experience, have we shared our story? There is value in "posting" our biblical past; each of us is uniquely designed by the Creator with gifts He endows for service in His kingdom. Beginning with our faith's baby steps and continuing in its maturity, we have stories that speak to the goodness of the Lord, of His love and faithfulness, of His making a way when all paths seemed blocked, of saying "Yes" when the doctor said "No," of His mercy and His grace. We have as did Paul "Throwback" vignettes to share as encouragement and enlightenment for fellow believers. The contemporary Thursday Throwback postings bring smiles, shaking of the head, the occasional, "Those were the days!" But the Christian lifestyle demands more than that; it requires Sunday through Saturday Throwbacks; one day is insufficient to tell the story of how great is the God we serve. So back to my beginning question: Is there value in this concept of sharing our past? Unequivocally YES! We believers can raise the bar of this newest trend; we can systematically share the good news of the gospel by "posting" what God has done for us as encouragement to strengthen others. And not just on Throwback Thursday, but every day!

30

OUTSIDE THE BOX

"...but whoever wishes to be great among you must be your servant...just as the Son of Man came not be served but to serve, and to give his life a ransom for many."
Matthew 20:26–28

In the late 1960s and early 1970s, the business world introduced a phrase that has since become somewhat of a cliché: 'Think outside the box." It was used by management to encourage workers to solve problems by thinking beyond the usual paradigms. Even today the British English Dictionary's definition of the idiom holds sway: 'to think imaginatively using new ideas instead of traditional or expected ideas.' And it is easily a concept that describes both Jesus' teachings in New Testament times and the abiding principles of those teachings Christians are called to follow today. I can imagine him smiling back in the day when the idiom became the catch-phrase at managerial levels within public and private enterprises —his way of thinking making inroads in the secular!

Jesus' words in this chapter of Matthew come after two disciples and their mother approach him with a request: *"Grant that one of these two sons of mine may sit at your right and the other at your left in your kingdom."* You know mothers and their sons; mom is always the number one fan and loyal supporter! As can be expected, this request for favor and recognition outraged the other disciples! "Say what? No, you didn't go there! Who do you guys think you are?" Pressed into immediate mediation mode, Jesus called them together and introduced 'outside the box' thinking for the first time in human history. Despite his teachings up to that point, it was obvious their concept of Jesus' kingdom was a traditional one, full of pomp with its trappings and of course privilege and rank. We can imagine the bewilderment and perhaps scratching of heads as he exclaimed the scripture above.

The very idea that he came to earth as a Servant Messiah, not to be served, but to serve and give his life as a ransom was definitely "outside the box." And as this concept challenged the disciples and other believers of that time, so it challenges believers today. Yes, we understand the basics of our commitment to follow Him in a similar life of service, especially to those less fortunate than we are. And we do try (my son would offer at this point that therein rests our problem: we "try" when we should "do"—but that's a piece for another day), but the temptations to put aside serving others and enjoy the perks of being served are just so appealing. I mean what's wrong with being recognized, deferred to, put on a pedestal, your needs being attended to without you asking, offered the best seat in the house, not having to wait with the crowd but being ushered to the front of the line? Isn't that what the good life is about and the scriptures do say that if we follow Him, He will bless us beyond what we can imagine. Aren't the perks just blessings after all? If Jesus' teachings had not been the consummate "outside the box" thinking, such ideas might have validity. But Jesus spoke and speaks still a radically different message, a message that is clearly nontraditional and unexpected. He declares that the selfless life style is the preferred life style; the mindset that the needs of others are not afterthoughts, but our primary consideration in the use of our talents and resources; that turning the other cheek when someone strikes us rather than striking back is the right thing to do; that if our enemy is hungry we are to feed him and if he's thirsty to give him something to drink; that offering to the one who wants our tunic, our cloak as well; that we are to love not just those who love us, but also our enemies and pray for those who persecute us; that we are to give to the poor and those in need without fanfare; that we are not to place value on our material possessions or store them up, but to share our wealth and bounty with those who have less than we do.

Had Jesus not come with an "outside the box" theology, and simply blended with the status quo religious mentality of his day, how different the faith we proclaim as Christians would be. But isn't it appropriate that the God we serve would have gathered those in the founding firm and taught them this innovative way of thinking, this blueprint for the future of the church; a blueprint that some 2000 years later keeps in proper perspective who we are as followers of Jesus—servants who serve because he served first. We can do no less.

Part Three

In — Not Of

Do not conform any longer to the pattern of this world, but be transformed by the renewal of your mind.

Romans 12:2

For though we live in the world, we do not wage war as the world does.

2 Corinthians 10:3

If you are a reader of **Our Daily Bread,** perhaps you read the story of the South African man who surprised nine home invaders inside his house. According to the account, seven ran away and the homeowner shoved the other two into his swimming pool. Now this is where the story gets interesting. One of the thieves could not swim, so the homeowner jumped in and rescued him. The fellow expressed his gratitude by calling out for his cohorts to return, pulling out a knife and threatening the homeowner with it. As they were still near the pool, the homeowner wisely pushed the culprit back into the water. Now at this point, you're thinking conventional wisdom is about to kick in. No more heroics; just a quick call to the authorities to end this drama. That unfortunately or fortunately, depending upon your view is not what transpired next.

The no swimming bad guy again began to struggle in the water and apparently forgetting what had just happened, the homeowner jumped again into the pool and rescued his potential attacker.

In—Not Of

The homeowner's actions give us pause because what he did is difficult to comprehend. Most of us would have not attempted a rescue, feeling the man deserved whatever happened to him. And we most definitely would not have dived back in the second time considering the attacker's response to our first rescue. The fellow's lack of gratitude and thanksgiving for saving his life, which ought to have prompted a change in his spirit, would have hardened our hearts to his plight. Our concern at that point would be the 911 call.

As I thought about this incident, it was clear what most consider conventional wisdom and logical thinking collided with the teachings of Jesus as recorded in the Gospel of Luke. In chapter six, Jesus speaks of loving our enemies, praying for those who mistreat us, turning the other cheek for those who strike us and even stripping our garments to give to those who take from us. We are instructed to treat them as we would wish to be treated even if they don't reciprocate. I'm thinking this homeowner's spirit of compassion sprang from his belief that these teachings must be lived, not just read. I am humbled and impressed as I read of a believer who apparently is not transformed by how the world thinks he should act.

Being a disciple of Jesus Christ is not for the faint hearted; and nor is it superficial. Those who profess Christ will make decisions that fly in the face of conventional wisdom and commonly accepted norms of behavior. The test of our faith may indeed require responses and sacrifices the world thinks foolhardy. But it is at these difficult and defining moments that we are called to remember we are in the world, not of it.

2

Seasons

There is a time for everything, a season for every activity under the heaven...

Ecclesiastes 3:1

The story of Moses keeps returning to me. I sense God trying to get my attention. What is it about this servant of the Lord that I need to understand better? Perhaps it's the fact that his life is easily divided into three stages or seasons. In his first forty years, he was raised in the royal courts of Egypt as the son of Pharaoh's daughter after she rescued him as an infant. He was the grandson of the Pharaoh himself. The book of Acts reads in chapter seven, verse twenty two, "Moses was educated in all the wisdom of the Egyptians and was powerful in speech and action." Born to a Hebrew mother during the time when the king had ordered the slaughter of all infant Hebrew males, he had little in common with those of his biological heritage during this season of his life. But God had His plans for this commoner raised an aristocrat. At birth he was "set apart" for God's express purposes. As a mature adult, wielding easily the privileges of royalty, Moses decides to champion the rights of the enslaved people. "He saw an Egyptian beating a Hebrew, one of his own people. Glancing this way and that and seeing no one, he killed the Egyptian and hid him in the sand." (Exodus 2:11–12)

Fear of retribution for his deed sets the stage for the next forty years of his life as Moses goes from royal prince to desert herdsman of his father-in-law's flock. Little is written of his life during those years. We know he was married and had sons, and we know it bore no resemblance to life in the palace. Those were the humbling years; years that deflated any sense of privilege. Royalty holds no attraction for desert sheep. The significance of this forty year period becomes apparent when God himself commands the shepherd's attention with a burning bush that is not consumed. Those years in Egypt had provided the formal training and education which gave Moses a spirit of inquisitiveness and curiosity. Rather than fleeing in fear at the sight—an expected response of a simple shepherd—he investigates. *"So Moses thought, 'I will go over and see this strange sight—why the bush does not burn up.'"* (Exodus 3:3) The fulfillment of God's purposes for Moses' life unfolds over his final forty years as God uses him to carry out His divine plans for His people, the Israelites.

Perhaps the reason the saga resonates is the fact that it is not much of a stretch to see God acting in our lives in similar fashion. True, we probably will not live 120 years as did Moses, but we all will experience seasons. God has a plan for each of us and that plan evolves in stages. We may not always understand a season's purpose, but once the time for action God has been preparing us for arrives, we will be ready. We will discover each preceding season has prepped us for the one we're confronting. And we will, as did Moses, approach the unknown not in fear, but with the confidence that comes from knowing God has been with us all along.

3

Never Say Goodbye

> *"For I am convinced that neither death nor life, neither angels nor demons, neither the present nor the future, nor any powers, neither height nor depth, nor anything else in all creation, will be able to separate us from the love of God that is in Christ Jesus our Lord."*
>
> Romans 8:38–39

My son had movie passes for the preview showing of Disney's *Toy Story 3* movie. He asked me to take my grandchildren and their cousin because he had to work and could not go. Somewhat reluctantly I agreed. I had just spent the evening before with the entire crew at a premier showing of another popular kid movie and kind of felt the need for some quiet time alone. Boy, was I glad I agreed to go! The girls were well behaved, funny and endearing in their enjoyment of what turned out to be a great Disney film. It's one we'll purchase when it comes out on DVD. What appealed to me most was the story line. Andy, the lead human character in the animated film, was about to leave for college and the toys that had been part of his life since early childhood must now be donated, placed in the attic or thrown away. Only one of the toys, the cowboy Woody makes the cut for the box marked "College." Without revealing the entire plot, suffice it to say the toys bounce from one perilous adventure to another, fighting to survive this season of transition and change. As the film nears its conclusion,

Andy and his toys realize the break with the past is inevitable. Nothing stays the same forever, at least not in the human or human engineered domain.

As the kids chatted happily on our way home, I reflected upon how blessed we are that as believers that is not our story. The God we serve and call friend never changes; His word is as true today as it was yesterday and will be tomorrow. We can count on Him to never outgrow us, as Andy did his toys. Yes, we too face times of change, uncertainty, tragedy and triumph. We call it living. But no matter our circumstances or the crisis of the moment, God does not ponder what box to place us in. He continues to love us, to forgive us and to shower us with His grace; even as one season of life folds into the next. As believers we have only to break with those things of the world that separate us from the Savior. We never have to say "Goodbye." Our God has promised to always be where we need Him to be: in our toy boxes, our rooms, our everywhere. He will never leave or forsake us, throw us in the trash or give us away. His love for us is constant and eternal. "Goodbye" is not in His lexicon.

4

Sage Dust

"And even the very hairs of your head are all numbered."
Matthew 10:30

"Sage dust," my high school friend called her ash grey closely cropped hair. "And I earned every bit of it. "We all laughed as we greeted one another with hugs and tears at our 50th high school reunion. I had not seen her since graduation day in May so very long ago. And yet when finally we recognized each other, it was as if time evaporated and we were 18 years old again. Effortlessly we resumed conversations halted by time and distances as if it was the next morning in the hallway of Lincoln High School and we were ambling to class together. There were ten of us then; a cliché you might say of virtuous, academically talented teen girls who bonded in a friendship that carried us through the four years of high school. Seven of us attended the weekend reunion, joyous to be in one another's company and with the others who comprised the Class of 1960.

My friend's comment about her closely shaved head came back to me when I returned home. I thought of Jesus' teachings that God knows everything about us, even the number of hairs on our head. He knew the number on her head before they turned grey and knows them even now that they are barely visible. Even the grey itself is a sign of His caring and blessing, an unmistakable measure of His grace and love. For reasons known to Him alone,

God has watched and cared for the seven of us who remain. With anyone who has been favored to see the sixth decade of life, we have known both the triumphs and tragedies life serves up. But oh, I am comforted with the certainty that a God who takes the time to number the hairs on our heads is a God who values us. Even when we may have thought He had forgotten us because our circumstances were so difficult, He was there; offering His comfort, His presence, His guidance so that we could be more than conquerors.

The words He spoke to our biblical ancestors echo through the ages. *"For I know the plans I have for you,"* declares the Lord, *"plans to prosper you and not to harm you, plans to give you hope and a future."* (Jeremiah 29:11) Those words still ring true, even in this later season of our lives. Who alone is worthy of our praise and thanksgiving? Only God, the creator and sustainer of life who knows the number of hairs on our head, from brown to grey, from the first to the last.

5

What? How? Why

Peter, however, got up and ran to the tomb. Bending over, he saw the strips of linen lying by themselves, and he went away, wondering to himself what had happened.

Luke 24:12

Does Peter's reaction upon peering into the empty tomb seem odd? Considering the teaching Jesus had done prior to His crucifixion about what He was about to endure and suffer, you'd think finding an empty tomb would have been a moment of epiphany! Instead, Peter who had been with Jesus at the Transfiguration and knew Him to be God's Son turned away in wonderment, trying to figure out why Jesus' body was not there. It's easy for us to find fault with this disciple upon whom Jesus had said He would build His church; for his seeming lack of faith in this juncture of his life after all he had witnessed Jesus do during their joint ministry, but that would be hypocritical. For who among us, like Peter, has not failed to recognize God's divine plans unfold in our own lives? We know what God's word says and yet our circumstances cause us to question and ponder "How? Why? What?" Like Peter, we fail to connect the dots; to relate what we see with what God has already told us He will do.

We see homelessness, poverty and despair amongst us; but His word declares, *"I was young and now I am old, yet I have never seen the righteous forsaken or their children begging bread."* (Psalm 37:25)

What? How? Why

We face unemployment, foreclosure or any number of financial challenges; but His word assures us, *"The righteous cry out, and the Lord hears them; He delivers them from all their troubles. The Lord is close to the brokenhearted and saves those who are crushed in spirit."* (Psalm 34:17–18) We see loved ones and friends bedridden with disease in hospitals and nursing care facilities, but His word promises, *"If any among you are sick, call the elders of the church to pray over him and anoint him with oil in the name of Jesus and the prayer offered in faithfulness will make the sick person well. The Lord will raise him up."* (James 5:14–15) And on the flip side, we may experience a season of overflowing favor and prosperity that cannot be measured. Even then His word speaks to us, *"Every good and perfect gift is from above, coming down from the Father of the heavenly lights, who does not change like shifting shadows."* (James 1:17)

The lesson is simple. Our days of Peter-like wonderment are over. For well over 2000 years Jesus has sat at the right hand of God our Father; taking His rightful seat there after His resurrection from the grave and ascension into Heaven. He is the intercessor who hears our prayers and responds as the Father so wills. We know the what, the why and the how because we know the Savior. There is no wonderment; the mystery is solved.

6

WHO IS MY NEIGHBOR?

"Love the Lord your God with all your heart and with all your soul and with all your strength and with your entire mind and love your neighbor as yourself."

Luke 10:27

The newspaper headline read, "Stabbed, Ignored Do-Gooder Buried." The article told of a man in New York City who was buried as a "Good Samaritan" after he was ignored by passersby as he lay mortally wounded on a city street after he had intervened in a dispute between and a man and a woman. His efforts cost him his life, even though he might have been saved had anyone stopped to assist. Immediately the biblical parable Jesus told thousands of years ago in the Gospel of Luke leaped to mind. In that passage, the gospel writer recounts an occasion when an expert in the law attempts to test Jesus by asking Him what one must do to inherit eternal life. Jesus answered him with a question. *"What is written in the Law?"* The lawyer responded with the verse as noted in Luke 10:27. Jesus told him he was correct and that he should go and do likewise. Seeking to justify himself, the lawyer parried, *"And who is my neighbor?"*

It was then that Jesus told the famous parable of the Good Samaritan. Most of us know the story of the Jewish man robbed, beaten and left for dead on the Samaritan Road. Both a priest and a Levite, an assistant to a priest, observed the wounded man and ignored him, going so far as to cross to the other side of the road to avoid him. But a Samaritan, a known adversary of the Jewish people, stopped to assist and render aid; even taking him to an innkeeper to convalesce and pay for his medical expenses. And promising to stop by on his way back to check and cover any additional costs incurred in the man's care. When Jesus ended the parable, He asked the expert in the law which of the three men was a neighbor to the injured man. He answered, "the one who had mercy on him." Jesus responded, "Go and do likewise." In other words, our adherence to the commandment to love our neighbor requires more than lip service. Jesus requires that we be "doers" of the word of God. The incident in New York City is sadly sobering in that it reminds us that many still choose to "pass by" or cross over to the other side rather than be a neighbor to the stranger in dire circumstances. Surely among those who for an hour according to the video tape of the incident looked but did not assist was at least one person who professes Christ! How painful to think if there were believers in the passersby, not even they stopped to offer comfort or render aid. Incidents such as this one remind us the more some things change, the more they remain the same. In this instance what has apparently not changed much is the lesson of this parable. Jesus' teachings of His expectations for those who follow Him are surely as relevant today as they were over 2000 years ago. His words were truth then; they remain truth today. May we be reminded daily to not turn a blind eye to injustice and truly to love as the Savior so commands so we may inherit eternal life.

7

Tomorrow

Pharaoh summoned Moses and Aaron and said, "Pray to the Lord to take the frogs away from me and my people, and I will let your people go to offer sacrifice to the Lord. Moses said to Pharaoh, "I leave to you the honor of setting the time for me to pray for you and your officials and your people that you and your houses may be rid of the frogs, except for those that remain in the Nile." "Tomorrow," Pharaoh said.

Exodus 8:8–10

The Pharaoh's response to God's intervention in his life is a classic example of the old saying: "putting off until tomorrow what ought to be done today." Here Moses has given the Pharaoh the choice to decide when the prayer would be offered that would bring relief to his situation and he decides to wait until tomorrow? Why? Can you imagine delaying even an hour to say nothing of a day to bring an end such an awful situation? Frogs in your bed? In your kneading trough where you prepare the bread you eat? Frogs everywhere! As incomprehensible as this biblical scenario seems, the Pharaoh's action of putting off until "tomorrow" what clearly needed to be done that day is even more bizarre.

But how often have we been like the pharaoh; delaying action when circumstances demand a decision now. How many times have we echoed him or perhaps even Scarlet O'Hara in the film *Gone with the Wind* who dealt with her challenges of the moment with the statement: *"I'll think about it tomorrow"*? Maybe Pharaoh had a logical excuse for telling Moses to delay praying for an end to the frog plague. After all he didn't believe in or worship God in the first place. And he had not the benefit of Jesus' teachings. But it's different for us; we know what the Scripture teaches: Do not boast about tomorrow, for you do not know what a day may bring forth. (Proverbs 27:1) Why, you do not even know what will happen tomorrow. (James 4:14) The reality is tomorrow is not promised. We have only the present moment to live in God's purposes. We seek His guidance and make decisions that allow His light to shine in us today. We choose adherence to those spiritual disciplines that bring us closer to Him today. We stop delaying behavioral changes we need to make today, not tomorrow. Why? The song "Tomorrow" by The Winans answers that question well, as it encourages listeners to accept the Lord today, because tomorrow isn't promised to any of us.

We must shun our human tendency to delay facing difficulties that challenge or confuse us. Today is the day we say "Yes" to decisions that reflect God's will and purposes.

8

INTERNAL CELL PHONE

People were also bringing babies to Jesus to have him touch them... Jesus called the children to him and said, "Let the little children come to me, and do not hinder them, for the kingdom of God belongs to such as these. I tell you the truth; anyone who will not receive the kingdom of God like a little child will never enter it."
Luke 18:15–17

Out of the mouths of babes—that old saying came to mind the other day after a dear sister friend shared a "grandmother story." Seems her three year old granddaughter was scrambling to heed the car pool driver's call to hurry; it was time to leave. The three year old was slowed in her response because as she explained to the harried adult, "I have to get my cell phone." Later in the day when her mother asked her why getting her cell phone (which I assume was a toy model, but in this day and age of digital access having become almost a birth right may have been the real deal) was so important, she answered clearly and without hesitation, "I needed it to talk to God." Priceless!

A ring of wisdom suitable to all of us who profess to be in personal relationship with the Lord. Certainly we would profit by making sure we have our "cell phones" with us to talk to God as we begin our day. Like this precocious three year old, we should understand we can't leave home without taking our connection to God with us. In fact, we really ought to go one step further and set

Internal Cell Phone

up a speed dial so that we can connect to the Savior as quickly as possible. "What? Are you suggesting we really program a number to God in our cell phones! What would that number be? That's the silliest thing I've heard today!"

Oh, I know; the reality is that on our man-made devices we can't literally speak to God. But remember. The creator of the universe and all within it provided instant access to Himself long before any such ideas related to communication via a device ever entered the mind of Alexander Graham Bell. We have an internal cell phone; it is housed in our hearts where it can't get misplaced and we don't have to look for it. His divine alternative to the three year old's digital device enables us to connect to Him in the twinkling of an eye. We can call Him up without taking our hands off the steering wheel of the car, without putting the baby down, without stopping anything in which we are engaged at the moment.

As we scramble to begin each day, like the three year old, we can "talk to God" by opening our hearts, hitting His number and connecting on the spot to Him. If you listen closely, undistracted by whatever is going on in your midst, you will hear Him say, "This is the day that I have made. Rejoice and be glad in it. And by the way, have a great day! Call if you need Me."

9

21ST CENTURY PERSECUTION

"Blessed are those who are persecuted because of righteousness.... Remember the words I spoke to you: No servant is greater than his master. If thy persecuted me, they will persecute you also."
Matthew 5:11, John 15:20

The article reported the experience of a college student who two years earlier was not allowed to speak as a valedictorian of her high school class because in her remarks she would have given God credit for her success. Where the other speakers thanked teachers or coaches, this young woman wanted to acknowledge that it was God who helped her get through high school. She took her case to court and the judge admitted it was the student's desire to attribute her achievements to her belief in God that resulted in the court's decision to deny her the opportunity to speak at her graduation ceremony. 21st century persecution for sure! Too often we modern day "saints" forget that the cross we have chosen to carry was never intended to be lightly borne. For many of us our declaration of faith is seldom tested because we travel too "closely to the shore," avoiding the deep waters that might require bold witness of our beliefs and allegiance to God alone. This student's unabashed desire to give credit where credit was due is commendable. Her experience serves to remind us that we should expect persecution for our belief in God in this era of ungodliness.

On this walk with the Savior, we should stump our toes rather often as we boldly proclaim our Christian principles and seek to live them in every circumstance. Rather than the isolated, infrequent news feature, such experiences ought to dominate the headlines. If the opposite is the norm, few reported instances of persecution of followers of Christ, what does that say about us? Perhaps we professed disciples are ignoring opportunities to witness to our beliefs. Jesus' words are clear: *"If anyone would come after me, he must deny himself and take up his cross daily and follow me."* (Luke 9:23) Into each of our lives ought to come some degree of persecution for our faith in God and what that faith requires of us. As we continue to live in and for Him, may we grow bolder in our witness. And may we forgo our tendency to avoid conflict with the world because our faith beliefs are in opposition to it.

10

Ageless Provision

"If anyone does not provide for his relatives, and especially for his immediate family, he has denied the faith and is worse than an unbeliever."

I Timothy 5:8

The devotional I read posited that our failure to care for our aged population violates the commandment God gave to "honor your father and mother." The writer suggested that our society does a negligible job in caring for the elderly. On the surface it is easy to agree. Many people in their seventies, eighties and nineties and older are left to fend for themselves or warehoused in questionable senior citizen facilities by families unwilling or unable to support them at home.

But a new phenomenon has begun in the recent decade. More and more we witness just the opposite occurring: aging and aged parents being called upon to support adult children and their families. The paradigm has shifted as increasing numbers of young and prime age adults find themselves underemployed or unemployed and subsequently dependent upon parents or grandparents. What are we to discern from this seemingly upside down state of affairs?

Paul's letter to his protégé, Timothy urged the faith community to specifically care for the needs of the widows and all family members. Perhaps we are to understand from this teaching just what verse eight of the fifth chapter of I Timothy says, "Provide for relatives..." Ages notwithstanding, relatives of the faithful are called to be supportive of one another. The economics of today are vastly different than in the time when Paul wrote these words regarding providing for relatives. Often now it is the older generation whose resources may be more stable that finds itself in the role of "provider." And often too these older family members welcome the company and support the younger generations offer when their resources are combined for the greater good of them all.

Today's faith community must be open both to God's word and the spirit behind His words. And that spirit says to us, that irrespective of age, we are one another's keepers. Our history as people of faith recalls that such living arrangements and generational family support was the norm, rather than the exception centuries ago. And as we are prone to say on many occasions, history has its way of repeating itself. Maybe this is the season and the time we are called to provide even more as God directs; caring for one another as relatives following the One who is the supreme provider of good gifts to us all.

11

No Shame

"If anyone is ashamed of me and my words in this adulterous and sinful generation, the Son of Man will be ashamed of him when he comes in his Father's glory with the Holy angels."
Mark 8:38

I had set off on an afternoon walk when I noticed a car moving slowly down the street. The driver made the block and on her return slowed to a stop, rolled down her window and with a big smile said, "I'm sorry. I was looking for an address and realize it must be on the other end of Westbourne." Before I could acknowledge her comment, she continued. "I'm Jehovah's Witness; I have a magazine I'd like you to read." I smiled, shook my head in the negative and replied, "No, thank you." Still smiling herself, she said, "Okay, enjoy your walk."

I thought of that young woman today when I read Jesus' words to his disciples and those gathered to hear His teachings as recorded in the gospel of Mark. She displayed no shame at all in sharing her faith concepts. Openly, in an unpredictable encounter with a stranger, she attempted to open a door to discourse about her beliefs. And she did it unselfconsciously with a cheerful countenance and pleasant manner. Now I don't happen to agree with her denominational beliefs, but I applaud the ease with which she and others of that denomination make an effort to share them. No one can accuse them of being ashamed of what they profess spiritually.

No Shame

This encounter during an afternoon walk made me raise the questions: Can I or others like me in the Christian faith make a similar claim? Do we extend ourselves to the stranger in any circumstance for the express purpose of sharing the good news of the gospel of Jesus Christ and His teachings and commandments? Do we carry with us tangible resources that we might give to someone we meet who does not know Jesus as their personal Savior? And does our countenance when we engage strangers reveal our joy in knowing Him as Lord of our lives? I can't speak for anyone except myself and I confess I too often fall short in this public manifestation of my faith.

Not that I think I'm ashamed of Jesus, far from it. But like too many of my fellow believers I am not as proactive in spreading God's word (as He himself told His disciples to do in His Great Commission) as was this young woman. My admission begs yet another question for the faithful: Is being ashamed of Jesus and not being proactive in sharing His word as we believe it one and the same? As we ponder these queries, may we grow in our courage to speak of our faith convictions openly to those we encounter; and may we discard our hesitancy to do so, using as an excuse "waiting for the right time" in favor of seizing every opportunity that presents itself to do so. The unashamed stranger in the car certainly did!

12

Pray First

Then the King said to me, "What is it you want?" Then I prayed to the God of heaven and I answered the king...

Nehemiah 2:4–5

In this historical book of the Old Testament, Nehemiah was at the time serving as the cupbearer to the Persian King, Artaxerxes. He had recently received word of the awful conditions the exiles were facing in Jerusalem. The news caused him to weep, fast and pray. As Nehemiah went about his cupbearer duties, the king noticed Nehemiah's sadness of spirit and asked the question noted in the scripture above.

Notice that Nehemiah did not respond instantly to the king's inquiry. Instead he prayed first to God. Only after lifting his concern to God did he answer the king. Now the passage doesn't give us Nehemiah's exact words at that moment, but we imagine he sought God's guidance. We draw this conclusion because of how he responded when he first received word about the plight of the people in Jerusalem as recorded in the beginning of the chapter. He prayed.

If only we could imitate Nehemiah! How beneficial would this spirit of "praying first" be as we face the myriad of decisions inherent in living day to day? Think for a moment of our typical responses and actions when questions or decisions demand answers. Even though we profess Christ and acknowledge Him as Savior, do we demonstrate this when it's "answering" or decision making time? How often do we "pray first?"

We have been socialized to think when confronted with problems to figure out the answers ourselves; to rely first and foremost upon our own abilities and resources. Praying about everything before responding is not automatic, except perhaps in truly horrendous circumstances. But in the day to day, in the mundane, we do not typically pause to pray first. Nehemiah models for us what it means to be a "first responder" in our faith. Our first response ought to be one of prayer, seeking the Lord's face, His guidance before moving into action of word or deed.

We cannot say how much time elapsed between the king's question to Nehemiah and his answer. It doesn't appear to have been that long. But we remember that effective prayer is not judged by its length, but rather by its fervency and sincerity. And if like Nehemiah we are going about our everyday responsibilities in right relationship with God, easily bringing our concerns to Him, we ought to automatically seek His guidance and the answers to our questions when trouble rears its head. At the moment that a question needs an answer or a decision demands a response, no matter the degree of urgency, we pause to pray first before we proceed. May we like Nehemiah possess the wisdom to go to God first in everything.

13

Little Billy Wisdom

"You are the light of the world…, let your light shine before men that they may see your good deeds and praise your Father in heaven."

Matthew 5:13–16

Need a sure plan for beginning your day? Begin with prayer, pause for quiet time and reflection with God, read your Bible and a devotional or two (or three!) and cap it off with the comics. Yes, I said the comics, those strips that we called the "funny papers" when I was a child. After biblical nourishment and refreshment and quiet time in the Lord's presence, nothing jumpstarts your day's adventures like a few good laughs generated by the print comedians. It's not unusual to find as I do that the comics will put you in deeper touch with your faith.

Consider a *Family Circus* offering: Grandma asks her grandson, *"How did you find school today, Billy?"* He answers, *"I just got off the bus and there it was."* Children are usually very literal. As I chuckled over Billy's understanding of grandma's question, I thought perhaps we miss the Lord's point on many occasions because we don't take His words literally. More often than not we filter them to fit what we think He meant or what we are most comfortable hearing. Unlike little Billy, we don't accept His words at face value.

Reflect for a moment on these words of the Savior. *"Love your enemy and pray for those who persecute you."* (Matthew 5:44) *"…*

do not worry about your life, what you will eat or drink; or about your body, what you will wear… do not worry about tomorrow, for tomorrow will worry about itself. Each day has enough trouble of its own." (Matthew 6:25, 34) *"Not everyone who says to me, 'Lord, Lord' will enter the kingdom of heaven, but only he who does the will of my Father who is in heaven."* (Matthew 7:21)

I could go on and on. The Bible is filled with Jesus' words that are intended to guide our lives. There is no need to paraphrase them; there is only a need to understand them as He spoke them. We need to be little "Billys" who hear the word and respond literally to what it says to us. We need to be as Jesus says in Matthew 18:3: *"I tell you the truth, unless you change and become like little children, you will not enter the kingdom of heaven."* Oh, that we might grow in allowing the little Billy in each of us to hear God's word and respond accordingly.

14

21ST CENTURY HOSPITALITY

Do not forget to entertain strangers for by so doing some people have entertained angels without knowing it.

Hebrews 13:2

A dear friend's experience raised the question of how we apply the teaching of this "hospitality" passage in the book of Hebrews to the times in which we live. Her experience also prompts us to ask, "What is Christian hospitality? How do we express it?"

Responding to a message left on her answering machine, my friend returned the call to discover a stranger on the end of the line. The caller identified herself as someone who knew Dianna's husband who was at the time the pastor of a church in the Los Angeles area. She had called to ask if the pastor and his family would assist her young adult daughter. The young woman was coming to the city for a casting call and needed transport from the airport as well as help securing affordable lodging. After conferring with her husband, they discovered the caller had made a mistake and called the wrong number. The person she thought she had contacted had the same name as the pastor. He cautioned her not to prolong the contact as this was someone they did not know, a stranger.

She did just the opposite. Not only did she contact the caller again, but also offered to provide transportation and lodging in her home for the daughter while she was in the city. Over the cries of alarm raised by her family, she extended the gift of hospitality for several days to this stranger! When she eventually shared this experience with some of us, our response was, "Only you would do something like that!" Then the "what ifs" started. It was difficult indeed to appreciate what she had done—opening her home to a complete stranger and possibly putting the safety and welfare of her family on the line—in light of the times in which we live. Most of us have no problem giving to the stranger within the context of an organization, but we hesitate to literally "open our door" to those we don't know. But my friend did just that. Like Abraham, she offered true hospitality.

In his epistle to the believers in Rome, the apostle Paul wrote, *"Share with God's people who are in need. Practice hospitality."* (Romans12:13) The young woman was in need of shelter and transportation, as well as food. My friend met all of those needs and demonstrated that we who profess Christ are called to a higher standard of living than that set by the world. We not only claim our faith, but we live it as a way of pointing others to Christ. Our continuing prayer is for God give us spirits of hospitality so that we miss no opportunity to offer it to those in need.

15

The Human Condition

"Pray that the Lord your God will tell us where we should go and what we should do."

Jeremiah 42:3

I urge anyone with a desire to understand the human condition to study God's word as recorded in the Bible. Within those pages, those who seek guidance and insight are sure to find it. Thus were my musings as I read the book of Jeremiah. In the forty second and forty third chapters, a remnant of the people who had not been seized by the conquering armies of Babylon approached the prophet Jeremiah and asked him to pray to God the verse quoted above. When the prophet agreed to pray to God as they had requested, the people added, *"Whether it is favorable or unfavorable, we will obey the Lord our God..."* (Jeremiah 42:6)

Caught in the most desperate of situations, the people sought God's deliverance by seeking His direction; appropriate actions for anyone when a way out of trial or tribulation is obscured by fear and doubt. And as He always does, God heard and responded to Jeremiah with a word of hope for the people. He told them clearly what He wanted them to do; He went a step further and even told them the consequences if they failed to follow the guidance they asked of Him and He gave.

Often we wonder why we continue to face challenges after we have prayed for the Lord's intervention and His guidance. If we

The Human Condition

are like our biblical ancestors, and I suggest we are, the answer may be found in our response to God when we confront, "what thus says the Lord." Because the answer Jeremiah gave was not what the people wanted to hear, they accused him of lying. And instead of following God's instructions, they disobeyed and followed their own desires. Aren't we just like that? When the answer doesn't come soon enough or it comes wrapped in the unfamiliar or not as we asked, we typically go our own way. We may not accuse anyone of lying to us, but we abandon the Lord's wisdom when it seems not to serve our purposes. Like these people of ancient times, we harden our hearts to a word from the Lord.

And therein the human condition stands. How often when the times are the toughest, when we ought to acknowledge our need for the Savior do we instead turn away from Him? And why do we turn away? Because we think we know better than He does what the answer from Him ought to be. The psalmist sings to the people, *"Today, if you hear his voice, do not harden your hearts as you did at Meribah…"* (Psalm 95:7–8) The writer of Hebrews cautions, "So, as the Holy Spirit says: *'Today, if you hear his voice, do not harden your hearts as you did in the rebellion, during the time of testing in the desert…"* (Hebrew 3:7–8) The human condition is often doing what we shouldn't; turning away from rather than toward God's counsel, hardening our hearts to His words, and in the end suffering the consequences.

16

The Christian Shuffle

"And now these three remain: faith, hope and love. But the greatest of these is love."

I Corinthians 13:13

In one of his devotionals, Oswald Chambers poses the question: "What difference has my salvation and sanctification made? For instance, can I stand in the light of I Corinthians 13, or do I have to shuffle?" (*My Utmost for His Highest*) Great attention-getting queries for a follower of Jesus Christ, aren't they? After all, if our salvation and sanctification haven't made any differences in our living, then what was the purpose for confessing Christ in the first place? In his declaration of the greatest gift, the apostle Paul wrote the famous "Love" passage in the thirteenth chapter of I Corinthians. Many of us can recite the verses. *"…and if I have not love, I am nothing. Love is patient, love is kind. It does not envy; it does not boast; it is not proud. It is not rude; it is not self-seeking; it is not easily angered; it keeps no record of wrongs. Love does not delight in evil but rejoices with the truth. It always protects, always trusts, always hopes, and always perseveres."*

Oh my! It is at this point that many of us are forced to admit we've become experts at what I term "The Christian Shuffle," that dance of hit and miss steps we execute even better than we do the steps of the Cupid Shuffle at wedding receptions. Depending upon our mood and the players involved in exasperating situations,

The Christian Shuffle

we may exhibit patience. Our more familiar cry at these times is "Lord, give me patience and give it to me now!" Most of the time we really do try to be kind; unless someone rubs us the wrong way and we forget how to spell kindness, let alone practice it. Maybe we have envy under control, but it's darn hard not to boast of the kids or grandkids' latest achievements or strut with pride when we're receiving some accolade or recognition. And perhaps the hardest for us to master is our anger issue. So many things seem to deliberately drive us to the anger zone that we typically concede defeat, utter words we can't take back and pray for forgiveness after the verbal explosion.

Yes, in all honesty, we have to admit we've gotten pretty good at this Christian Shuffle. We do far more of it than we do of standing in the light of our salvation and sanctification. As believers and followers of Jesus, mindful of this great teaching in Paul's letter to the church at Corinth, we must resist this notion of shuffling (except those steps at the wedding reception!). We are called to a higher standard; one that demands a stationary stance and leaves the "Christian Shuffle" to those new on the dance floor of faith.

17

PEACEMAKER OR PEACEKEEPER
WHICH ARE YOU?

"Blessed are the peacemakers for they will be called the children of God."

Matthew 5:9

Until I read a recent devotional, I had never thought about the difference between the terms peacemaking and peacekeeping. Like many, I considered them synonymous. Upon reflection, I realize that they are not. Peacekeeping implies passivity whereas peacemaking suggests a more active posture.

Peacekeeping avoids conflict by maintaining as much as possible the status quo. It is a passive posture that seeks not to bring about peace, but to maintain an appearance of peace at any cost. Peacekeeping is "politically correct." Those who advocate and practice it are careful not to step on toes, to do nothing that might raise the ire of competing factions. In our time, peacekeeping has become the diplomatic approach. So what if atrocities are being committed, if justice is a joke, if human rights violations are wrapped in a flag of national sovereignty; peacekeepers tread lightly to avoid what may develop into circumstances that spin out of control.

What the world needs and Jesus elevates is the idea of peacemakers. These "children of God" are active in their pursuit of righteousness, justice and mercy. Unafraid to confront societal norms or national ideologies, peacemakers seek solutions that transform conflicting opinions into positions that can work for the common good. Peacemakers are never content with the way things are as long as opposing views prevent progress for all. Peacemakers do everything possible to promote relationships that are conflict free, remembering that scripture advises, *"He must turn from evil and do good; he must seek peace and pursue it."* (I Peter 3:11)

Peaceful relationships between individuals within any grouping – families, workplaces, communities, nations—do not happen unless someone makes an effort to produce them. Peacemaking is active and purposeful. It is the standard Jesus gives us for how we are to live in relationship with one another. Scripture tells *"If it is possible, as far as it depends on you, live at peace with everyone."* (Romans 12:18) When it isn't possible, we move from being peacekeepers to peacemakers by pursuing peace as children of God.

18

RESISTANT SURRENDER

"If anyone would come after me, he must deny himself and take up his cross and follow me…"

Mark 8:34

Who will admit with me the ongoing challenge of full denial of self, i.e. surrender to Jesus? Though I say it, I sing it, I pray it, I'm not sure I do it primarily because my struggle is with what total denial and surrender to Christ really means. This is not a confession a declared follower of Jesus easily makes. But the first step toward obedience is admission that one is not obedient, at least not totally. Jesus words are clear enough. In the Gospel of Luke He states, *"No one who puts his hand to the plow and looks back is fit for service in the kingdom of God."* Heavy stuff by any stretch of the imagination. The dictionary defines the verb surrender to mean "giving oneself up into the power of another; to yield." It offers as a synonym the word "relinquish." I don't propose to speak for my fellow strugglers, but I confess my issue is tied more to the synonym. I believe I have yielded myself to God's power; I don't have a problem with this aspect of my faith. I understand that my salvation rests upon my acceptance of Jesus as my personal Savior, that His atonement for my sins is what gives me an assurance of God's faithfulness and grace.

I think where I struggle is with the notion of "relinquishing." There are behaviors and attitudes that I have not surrendered or relinquished to God. And it is those behaviors and attitudes I hold on to that block full surrender. Denying yourself and taking on kingdom issues fly in the face of what most of us strive for, i.e. comfortable living and the nicer amenities such living affords for ourselves and our loved ones. Total surrender to kingdom building would mean relinquishing all but the basic necessities and using most resources for the work to which Jesus calls us. Further, total surrender requires no looking back wistfully for those things we sacrifice or envying them in others.

So I come full circle. Acutely aware of my shortcomings in this area and understanding from Jesus' words that I have no other option, my task is clear. Each day must be one in which I intentionally reject what clutches me and impedes my submission to Him. I know the tools He has given me to become the surrendered follower: continuous, fervent prayer, time in His presence studying and meditating upon His word, listening for His quiet whisper, recognizing His gentle nudge to go in one direction rather than another, to make this choice and not that one. Obedience to each will position me to surrender without faltering. The decision to do so is mine. There is no other if I am truly to be called His follower.

19

Reluctant Servant

But Jonah was greatly displeased and became angry... But the Lord replied, "Have you any right to be angry?"... God said to Jonah, "Do you have a right to be angry about the vine?" "I do," he said. "I am angry enough to die."

Jonah 4

This particular biblical ancestor has always intrigued me. Jonah seemed a most unlikely character for God's purposes. He was certainly no Isaiah, eager to go for the Lord wherever he was sent. No, Jonah was what I call a "reluctant servant." If you recall the story, it was only after he suffered the consequences of his disobedience (trapped inside the belly of a fish just might make you reconsider your response!) did he decide that perhaps he ought to follow through with God's plan. But aren't we just like Jonah in many instances? How many times have we gone our own way, refusing to follow God's guidance, only to come back to Him pleading for rescue when we are drowning in our dire circumstance? And of course at those moments we promise to do whatever He wants us to do.

Why, I wonder did God choose such a reluctant, angry person to preach to the people of Nineveh? Surely there was someone else more open and suitable to follow His commands. Maybe His choice lets us see that He can use even the hesitant spirit with shortcomings to achieve His purposes. In other words, we all have the potential to serve the Lord. Even if sometimes as in Jonah's case, we move into that service with an attitude problem.

Yes, we'll do what He says, but on our own terms. And the saga of Jonah shows us what happens when we do. Things don't work out and then we get mad at God! We seize the chance to confront Him as did Jonah: *"O Lord, is this not what I said when I was still at home? That is why I was so quick to flee to Tarshish."* And like Jonah, we sit and pout. Our spirit of obedience is tainted by our sense that God isn't fair after all.

But Jonah's story ends with God telling him essentially that He alone is in control of all He creates; He does what He does for His own purposes. In other words, the clay doesn't tell the potter what to do! We don't get a sense of what Jonah was thinking or feeling past that point in the narrative. But what we do we learn from their exchange is what our role is as disciples of the Lord. We serve without question; we allow God to bring whatever results he brings to our situations. We forgo anger and disillusionment, confident that God is in control. We praise Him for His faithfulness, even when we don't understand His actions.

20

Worry Anonymous

"Therefore I tell you, do not worry about your life…"Therefore do not worry about tomorrow…"
Matthew 6:25, 34

"Do not be anxious about anything…"
Philippians 4:6

One of my favorite comic strips is "Baby Blues." Almost always it speaks to the human condition with just the right touch of humor. Just this week, one of the strips was "spot on." In it the mother sits in bed reciting all the possible things that could go wrong with their children in the future. Wisely the father tells her to stop worrying because "there are things in life that you just can't control." With wide eyes zeroing in on him, mom responds in classic worrier fashion, "Yeah. That worries me too."

Though I have written before about the needlessness of worry, this comic strip reminded me of how difficult it is for us to give it up. It's as if we'd be lost if we didn't have something to worry about. Maybe our inclination to worry despite knowing it's pointless to do so comes from fear of living worry free. Imagine the paradigm shift of living each day undeterred by worry about anything; just trusting instead in the guiding hand of God. What freedom such a state would provide! Then we would have no excuse for not being about the Lord's business. And perhaps that's why we prefer to worry instead.

Worry Anonymous

Worrying fills the space in our minds and hearts and denies Faith room to have its way. If we are worrying, we can keep our hearts and minds turned inward to our issues. Worrying blinds us to the potential God gives us to make a difference and to glorify Him. Worrying keeps our faith in its infancy stage. Worrying is akin to saying, "Don't bother me now with that; can't you see I'm bogged down in worry with what to do about_____ (Fill in the blank yourself).

Now I know it's hard to live without being anxious about what I term the three F's: family, finances and future. But for believers in Jesus and the words of the Bible (our resource book I term *Living 101 through Advanced Living*), we can't say we trust God in one breath and have worry beads circulating in our minds and hearts at the same time. No, followers of Jesus give Faith power over every aspect of their lives. And though they may say, "My name is _____ and I am a worrier;" they can add to that disclaimer, "But it's been six months and counting since I worried about anything. I have given Faith permission to stop me any time I am tempted to worry. In prayer and supplication with thanksgiving, I go to God with everything and trust that He will show me the best way."

So Believer whether you just joined Worry Anonymous or have been a member all your life, stay the course with Faith as your "sponsor;" keep worry where it should be: trapped in the jar that overflows with joy.

21

Perversity

> *"Woe to those who call evil good and good evil, who put darkness for light and light for darkness, who put bitter for sweet and sweet for bitter."*
>
> Isaiah 5:20

I sat last evening watching a popular television police drama in a state of amazement. A man was on trial for child abuse. He defended his actions with the argument that he and others like him who indulged in such practices were themselves victims of society's laws that prohibited adult-minor love/sex relationships. He held the position that it was a violation of his civil rights and even claimed that the use of the term "pedophile" to describe him was akin to using the "N" word when referring to African Americans. Thankfully the jury rejected his spurious arguments, delivered a guilty verdict and sealed their decision with a coup de grace sentence: 3,000 years in prison for his crimes against children.

As the program credits rolled down the screen, I couldn't help wondering how such a subject could have even been explored on television. And then I remembered that such shocking issues have become a norm in the fabric of our modern society. Not to say that such practices are new to mankind's long history of abuse of the most vulnerable in its midst, but typically they have been topics about which one whispered or talked around. This brazen, in your face particular twist of evil is just further evidence of how

Perversity

far removed we are from God and His purposes for our lives. And though on first exposure such thinking may be shocking, it should not be for believers. We stand as contemporary witnesses to the fact that God's word has not lost its relevancy in our times. As it was for our biblical ancestors to whom the prophet spoke the words in the fifth chapter of Isaiah, it is for us. On every front we are exposed to evil, to man's desire to shape life for his own desires rather than those of God.

While the subject matter explored on the mainstream television show is utterly offensive to common decency, we are wise to remember that such is the tenor of the times. Followers of Jesus Christ are engaged in a battle that pits evil against good and too often, by the devil's craftiness, that evil is disguised as the opposite. We must be intentional in seeking God's guidance, His wisdom and most importantly His discernment. For it is only with these weapons that the faithful can stand firm in a world that too often seeks to redefine right and wrong, good and evil for its own purposes. The moral compass of our age is easily swayed; good and evil are twisted to suit man's desires and whims. Perversity must never lose its time honored meaning: *"turned away from what is right or good."* Any attempt to redefine that meaning cannot be tolerated.

22

THE LAW — THE ATONEMENT

We know that the law is good if one uses it properly.
                                                            I Timothy 1:8

As I read the first chapter of First Timothy, verse eight for some reason stuck in my mind. The Apostle Paul wrote these words to his protégé Timothy who was laboring for the Lord in the city of Ephesus at the time. Some of the believers were proving to be false teachers of the gospel by their misunderstanding of the Law. Paul's letter was an effort to direct Timothy's ministry in the right direction. Though he was not present when Jesus spoke about the Law during His sermon on the mount, Paul surely knew the essence of that message. Jesus was clear when He said, *"Do not think that I have come to abolish the Law or the Prophets; I have not come to abolish them but to fulfill them. I tell you the truth, until heaven and earth disappear, not the smallest letter, not the single stroke of a pen; will by any means disappear from the Law until everything is accomplished... For I tell you that unless your righteousness surpasses that of the Pharisees and the teachers of the law, you will certainly not enter the kingdom of heaven."* (Matthew 5:17–20) And though Paul's words may seem to lessen the importance of following the Law, in reality they point to an understanding of how the Law and Atonement of Christ work hand in hand. At least in my opinion.

What the Pharisees and faith communities then and now skip is Jesus' assertion that He was the fulfillment of the Law. The Law

The Law—The Atonement

pointed to Him; it set the standards for what was necessary to live righteously before God. That is what Jesus modeled. When He came in the flesh, He said in essence, "I am what you have been striving to be. I am the way to righteousness. Follow me." When the Law is used to give direction to Christ and to lay out the standards He represents, then it is properly used. When it is used to condemn and to judge it loses the purpose God intended.

He gave the Law to serve as a guideline, hoping that would be enough. All too soon, humanity showed that it was incapable of obedience to the Law. Jesus Christ's atonement for our disobedience allowed us another chance to be saved from our sins.

His atonement did not however take away our responsibility to follow the commandments and the law as a witness to our salvation. We don't get a "free pass" to sin because Jesus died on the cross at Calvary. Jesus expects us to go beyond the dictates of the Law of Moses and live in faith the Gospel He preached. We accept Him as the one without sin who was sent to earth by God the Father to atone for our inability to obey the Law and His teachings concerning the Law. Only when we obey His teachings in regard to both will our righteousness exceed that of those who hold to the Law alone as the ticket to eternity.

23

Two Roads

Enter through the narrow gate. For wide is the gate and broad is the road that leads to destruction, and many enter through it. But small is the gate and narrow the road that leads to life and only a few find it."

Matthew 7:13–14

I saw a picture today of a pathway that appeared to end in that proverbial, "fork in the road." As I stared at it, I first thought of an incident in a novel I was reading wherein one of the lead characters is at just such a divide on the trail he travels. He must decide whether to go to the right or to the left. He chooses the one path finally because to him it looked wider and more used. That decision turned out not to have been the wisest choice as he and his traveling companions almost lose their lives as a result of going that way. The tragedy of his decision was the fact that the less traveled, narrower road he rejected would have led them safely to their destination.

This rather long segue brings me to my point. As Christians we often come to places in our journey where the way forks and we must make a decision about which path to follow. Sometimes it's difficult because one choice seems not to be too much better than the other. Yet, if we deliberate as we pause to consider our choice and what our faith teaches, we will find the words of Robert Frost's poem, "The Road Not Taken," to be true indeed.

Two Roads

"I shall be telling this with a sigh somewhere ages and ages hence; two roads diverged in a wood, and I—I took the one less traveled by, and that has made all the difference."

The lesson is simple enough. The road to glory is not an eight lane interstate highway that runs across the county. No, the road to glory resembles more the two lane country road that meanders and has many forks; with each fork in the road offering its travelers options to consider. For a disciple of Jesus Christ, the choice should be obvious. If a road gives the appearance of being one many take, more than likely it's not the "narrow" road God favors. Because His followers are distinct, set apart from the world, the road they choose will be the one rejected by the crowd. Their choices will reflect a certain wisdom, a discernment, a faith that informs their decision about which is the better road.

Nurtured by the Word of God and prompted by the Holy Spirit, when Christian disciples come upon the forks that dot the landscape, they are more likely to choose the road "less traveled." They know it is best because they know the wisdom of Proverbs 3:5–6 —"Lean not upon your own understanding. In all your ways (even the act of choosing a road) acknowledge Him and He will direct your path."

24

Fiery Furnaces

> *Then King Nebuchadnezzar leaped to his feet in amazement and asked his advisers "Weren't there three men that we tied up and threw into the fire?" They replied, "Certainly, O King." He said, "Look! I see four men walking around in the fire, unbound and unharmed and the fourth looks like a son of the gods."*
>
> Daniel 3:24–25

Reflection upon the story of the three young men cast into the fiery furnace prompted the realization: fiery furnace experiences are common to anyone who pledges allegiance to God. When we attempt to live our convictions, we find ourselves cast over and over again into circumstances that have the power to consume us, much like the fire had into which the three young men were cast. In facing whatever challenges that come our way, we who say we are sold out for the Lord might look to their example. They knew who they were, to whom they belonged and they were grounded in their faith convictions. Their trust in the God they served was absolute; they did not waver or attempt to accommodate or please anyone except him.

Threats had no effect. Because their faith was beyond reproach and their trust level "off the charts," they could calmly respond to the king, *"If we are thrown into the blazing furnace, the God we serve is able to save us from it, and he will rescue us from your hand, O king. But even if he does not, we want you to know, O king*

Fiery Furnaces

that we will not serve your gods or worship the image of gold you have set up." (Daniel 3:17–18) Talk about holy boldness and being strong in your convictions of faith! It doesn't get any stronger and real than this declaration in the face of certain death. We know of no Christians today who are faced with literal fiery furnaces; but Christians who seek to live a faith-filled life will encounter challenges that test their faith. Trouble is no respecter of person. Natural and unnatural disasters befall any and all. Evil is real and can touch the lives of novice and seasoned saint alike. Amid these challenges, a response will be required. Will that response mirror the faith, trust and unwavering obedience of the young men in Nebuchadnezzar's furnace?

For far too many professed Christians the answer is NO. Often the opposite is our truth. We forget who we are and "going along to get along" better describes our responses. We comprise; we forget to whom we belong; we reinterpret God's word to more comfortably fit our lifestyles; we choose disobedience by ignoring what we term outdated theology; and we seek man's approval for our choices, rather than holding them up to the light of Christ. Alongside the furnace believers, we pale. O, that we might muster their courage, their faith, their conviction in our times of peril! O, that we might in the worst of times stand firmly upon the faith we profess.

25

Soul Man

I lift up my eyes to the hills—where does my help come from?
My help comes from the Lord, the maker of heaven and earth.
                                                    Psalm 121:1–2

The comments of fans who attended a concert that starred a well-known Rhythm and Blues female vocalist keep recurring to me. According to the newspaper writer who reviewed the performance and the crowd's reaction, the audience was wildly enthusiastic. Those who spoke to the journalist following the show shared how the star's music over the years had helped them weather the various life seasons. To paraphrase their comments, she had been there with them in song as they faced relationship issues, raised their children and battled the winds of adversity common to the human condition. Her music, they intoned, brought them through. As I concluded reading the article, I sighed. I am of that same generation as many of these women. I well remember the popular lyrics this soulful diva belted out and how those words had the power to speak to your inner struggles.

What I can proclaim now that I could not and did not during those decades of "groovin'" to her music is that there is someone whose music is even sweeter and smoother, whose lyrics speak to every imaginable circumstance known to man, and whose word power to lift, sustain and transform has no limitations. That someone is Jesus. His sweet and pure name is above every name that ever existed. And the lyrical words of hope, assurance and encouragement contained in His album of oldies and goodies—our Bible—are unparalleled and unequaled by any human songstress. It is sobering to think that some of us in my generation and many of our children and grandchildren are still caught up in secular sedatives to address the stresses and challenges of our lives. And rather than going to the master solace provider, the Man of Soul, Jesus Himself, we seek instead balms from other sources, including the music of popular lyricists. We forget when we turn to the secular that only Jesus' lyrics are ageless, filled with divine supernatural power to provide all we need or want. He is the balm that soothes the "sin sick soul." For all of us, from teenager to senior citizen, the time is past for looking for solace in all the wrong places. There is only one to whom we need go and His name is Jesus. He alone can and will provide strength and solace that will get us in and through the seasons of our lives.

26

Fixer Syndrome

Now, Sarai, Abram's wife, had borne him no children. But she had an Egyptian maidservant named Hagar; so she said to Abram "The Lord has kept me from having children. Go sleep with my maidservant; perhaps I can build a family through her."
Genesis 16:1–2

I offer a piece of advice, just a piece—surrender yourself to the Lord's time and purposes and avoid if at all possible the arrogance of being a "fixer" of the situations common to humankind. Reject the moniker—"Modern Day Sarai." You recall the biblical Sarai's story in chapter sixteen of the book of Genesis. On her own she decided to build a family her way rather than waiting on God to fulfill His promise. The result of her decision was disastrous. She had no idea what she was setting into motion and the long term consequences of her actions. Unto this day, the hatred, violence and conflict generated by her "fixer" efforts continue in the Holy Land.

Sarai's story is an example of what happens when we think we need to run God's business, to step into His domain. In our ignorance and arrogance, we forget we control nothing. Everything with which we have been blessed; everything by which we have been challenged, He foreknew and allowed. So when we seek to bring about what we think ought to occur; when we decide our plans trump God's, we shouldn't be surprised by the inevitable consequences. Without fail, they will come. And more often than not they will not be what we planned. Our arrogance can produce suffering, confusion, and a host of undesirable outcomes. And even when and if our circumstances settle into something we can manage, the price we will have paid or the pain we will have suffered or caused others to suffer remains. Life moves forward, but at what cost. As the lyrics of the old hymn declare, "Oh, what peace we often forfeit, oh, what needless pain we bear; all because we do not carry everything to God in prayer;" And having carried it there, waited on God to carry out His will.

Yes, my advice is simple: stop thinking you are in control of anything or of the ultimate outcome of any situation. You are not. Take your heart's desires to the Lord. Have your conversations with Him; trust His judgment and His time frame. Leave it at His altar. Accept that you don't need to carry baggage that belongs to Him. He's perfectly capable of carrying every load. Lead that "Sarai" spirit to the door; say adieu and throw the deadbolt. Let the winds carry it away. Surrender yourself totally to God. You'll cause a lot less damage when you do.

27

EVEN MARTHAS FINALLY GET IT

Jesus said to her, "Your brother will rise again." Martha answered, "I know he will rise again in the resurrection at the last day." Jesus said to her, "I am the resurrection and the life. He who believes in me will live, even though he dies; and whoever lives and believes in me will never die. Do you believe this?" "Yes, Lord," she told him, "I believe that you are the Christ, the Son of God, who was to come into the world."

John 11:24–26

When I read this scripture, I reflected upon two things. First, this is the same Martha who earlier in Jesus' ministry had complained to Him about her sister Mary's behavior during one of His visits to their home. You remember the incident. As Jesus sat teaching, Mary was at His feet listening to His every word while Martha busied herself with preparations. Frustrated that she alone was working, Martha appealed to Jesus to make Mary help, or in the words of the vernacular, "help a sister out." Jesus' responded that Martha was worried about the wrong things and Mary had chosen what was better, i.e. spending time listening to His teachings.

Now this same Martha was addressing Jesus with her belief that her brother would not have died if Jesus had arrived sooner and confessing her belief that Jesus was the Son of God, the resurrection and the life. Talk about a major transformation; this was one indeed! At some point in the time that elapsed between Jesus' admonition about what is truly important and the death of her brother, Lazarus, Martha's faith meter had risen dramatically. She could respond simply, "Yes, Lord, I believe."

And it is this moment in Martha's story that I make my second observation. Often, at the beginning of our spiritual journey, our knowledge of Jesus is superficial. Like Martha initially, we are so busy with secular concerns, we give little time to pause, listen, reflect and learn as the Master speaks. Our schedules are too jam-packed for spending time with our Bible and devotional resources. We think quiet time with God is for retired people or those who live in convents or monasteries. Every minute counts as we scurry from one activity to another.

But God has a way of breaking through our shell of resistance to get our attention. Not uncommonly it involves some pain, some unexpected challenge, something we'd rather not deal with, but over which we have no control. It is at these times, these moments that we finally stop to reconsider our relationship with Him. It's not a stretch to think that during the days in which she waited for Jesus to come after He received word that Lazarus was ill that she came to understand who He was and why she needed Him.

We are like that. We understand in times of crisis and challenge only He can help us weather the storm. We go to Him with our burdens; we confess Him as Lord and Savior; and when He whispers, "Do you believe I am the resurrection and the life?" we answer, "Yes, Lord, I believe."

Part Four
One Minute Reflections

Trust in the Lord with all your heart and lean not on your own understanding. In all your ways acknowledge Him, and He will make your paths straight.

Proverbs 3:5–6

Does life need to be complicated? Is its complexity necessary for us to understand our absolute need for God? I'm inclined to answer "Yes." I don't know about you but I find when I've finished my early morning devotional and prayer time and turn to the demands of my secular life, the engagement with family, friends and the world beyond, the serenity and peace I knew during my quiet time with the Lord slowly ebb. And as the hands on the clock move forward, chipping away at another 24 hours, so do the realities of life wear away the peace with which I began the day. By mid-morning or just after, it hits me that I cannot continue alone any longer. It is too much, too complex for me. I am at a loss. I recognize I cannot travel for even a few hours on this day's journey without God. I need His patience, His clarity, His direction, His "hands-on" guidance, wisdom and strength if I am to survive. If I had not the complexities each day brings, I might begin to believe I was in control; that I did not need my Savior. How dangerous such thinking would be! So bring on the complications, the complexities; they keep us where we need to be: totally surrendered and dependent upon God!

2

God keeps in perfect peace those whose minds are stayed (steadfast) on Him.

Isaiah 26:3

We have a tendency to forget His word of assurance and comfort, especially during times of crisis. Too often when our carefully constructed life collapses and our prayers for deliverance go unanswered, we go into panic mode. We despair and lament, *"My God, my God, why have you forsaken me? Why are you so far from saving me, so far from the words of my groaning?"* (Psalm 22:1–2) We allow our minds to drift away from Him because it seems He isn't responding to our needs. Our peace in His presence evaporates. And without that peace we cannot cope. We decide God has turned away and we fall deeper into despair. But what we are called to remember is it is exactly in those moments of despair that God speaks. To hear Him we must reorient our minds to where we find Him: in prayer and Scripture. That is where He is waiting to whisper to us words of comfort; to pass by with an extended hand of peace. When the way is darkest, be still and keep your mind stayed on Jesus. The perfect peace of which Isaiah writes is there. A mind steadfastly attuned to the Lord will know the peace only He gives.

3

"...in quietness and trust is your strength."

Isaiah 30:15

Sometimes our notion of "holding on" in our circumstances is not what Go is after. It can be that He desires us to "let go," despite our fear that in so doing, we will lose all, will fail and will forfeit everything. If we reflect upon our relationship with the Lord, we understand that dependency upon Him and submission to Him are the conditions He prefers. For with the "letting go" comes the necessity of trust. "Holding on" can taint the purity of our trust because it implies we think God is not sufficient. God seeks to break through that hesitancy we harbor as a hedge in our favor. It is not. In fact, hesitancy in trusting God in all things, in waiting with the expectation that in all our circumstances He is able, reveals the crack in our armor. The point of the lesson then is to seek discernment through prayer that says to us, "It's time to let go." God's got it! Only when we give it over to the Lord and fall away from it in trust does God provide the parachute to sustain us.

4

"...just as the Son of Man did not come to be served, but to serve, and to give his life as a ransom for many."
Matthew 20:28

Jesus came to earth as a servant Messiah. As such, He did not meet the expectations of the people who were looking for a royal Messiah to reestablish Israel's dominance. But as the passage in Matthew's Gospel reads, Jesus Himself declared that He did not come to be served, but to serve. Even with our post biblical insight, many followers of Jesus today still struggle with this concept of "servant leadership." We know that as disciples we are called to be like Him, to live the servant life of Christ as a mark of our faith. And although we try, too often we yield to the temptation to put aside serving others and embrace the perks of being served. We even justify ourselves with the observation that too often those we seek to serve are not appreciative and even think it their due to be on the receiving end of our services and our resources. No wonder that after a time as this mindset seals, the idea of selfless service gets to be a drag. "Let someone else attend the needs of the least, lost and last for a while. We need a break!" Aren't you glad Jesus didn't get to this point during His brief time of service as He walked the dusty roads of the Holy Land? Those He served didn't always accept His message or heed His call. Many took His healing powers as their due; if He had the power, then why not take advantage of it? Many received and went on their way. Even those who witnessed firsthand the miracles of His servant leadership did not accept Him as Messiah. But Jesus did not yield to any expectation than that of God the Father. His purpose was clear: to show by His service God's glory and power. Nothing has changed. Today, as disciples of Jesus Christ, we are called to respond to the world with the same qualities of service He modeled. We must resist the lure of looking only to our own needs and wants. We must extend ourselves and make available our resources to those who have less and who are without hope. True the rewards of service to others may never be realized. But we don't serve for reward or recognition. We serve because our Savior served and as His followers we can do no less.

5

Scripture tells us in Colossians 2:6–7 that as we have received Christ, we are to walk in Him as we have been taught. And Psalms 25:4–5 instructs us to follow the Lord's ways and paths. When we read these words they seem simple enough; walk in Christ and follow His ways and paths. Easy, right; well, not really. For some reason we struggle with these teachings. What I observe and in truth have been guilty of is yielding to the temptation to direct my journey irrespective of what the word of God says.

Once we accept Jesus' call and begin this journey with Him, we too quickly tug at His sleeve, insisting we really ought to turn here, or rest there, or take this shortcut we know about. Before we realize what we're doing, we have assumed His position as Life's Tour Guide. We maneuver Jesus over to the side on the path, still available if we need Him, but clearly no longer in charge of the journey. At this point, we are clearly no longer walking in Him, or allowing Him to show us His ways and paths. As disciples of Jesus, our charge is to actually practice what we've been taught. The testament of our faith is just that, our willingness to abandon our will to Him. Only when we discard our egos, our pride, our self-sufficiency and our self-centeredness in the trash barrels that line the pathways to glory will we walk in Christ. Total surrender and total reliance upon the author of our faith is the only way that will take us to eternity. Let us live the faith that we have been taught by the power of the Holy Spirit.

6

*His master replied, "Well done, good and faithful servant...
Come and share your master's happiness."*
Matthew 25:21

Imagine the joy of hearing those words spoken when you have finished the journey and completed the work God appointed to you. Most assuredly you will experience real, unsurpassed joy in that crowning moment when Christ welcomes you and acknowledges that you handled in a manner pleasing to Him the ministry in which you were engaged. At that moment, all the pain, all the suffering, all the doubts, fears and confusion will fade away. Only the joy of the Lord's accolades will resonate as you understand that "You did it!" You surrendered your will to God's and went about the kingdom service he required of you. Oh, you may for a moment recall it wasn't easy. The temptation to turn aside, to bury your talents, to ignore Jesus' call to service lurked in the shadows. But with prayerful discipline you stayed the course. You clung to the Master's promises. You saturated your mind and spirit with the tonic of His word. You endured; you pressed onward in faith; you kept your eyes on the prize. "Well done, good and faithful servant." There can be for the faithful no more soul-satisfying words than these from the Lord of our lives. Hallelujah!!

7

God will never leave or forsake us.
Deuteronomy 31:6–8

As God has been with others who believed in him, he will be with us. He will not forsake or leave us.
Joshua 1:5

God is with us and will not fail us nor forsake us until we finish the work he has given us to do.
I Chronicles 28:20

God will never leave nor forsake us so we are to be content with what we have and not lovers of the material.
Hebrews 13:5

The Bible overflows with God's promises to His followers. Perhaps the promises that offer the most comfort and strength are those noted in the preceding scriptures. Bottom line—God will not forsake us.

When the winds of adversity blow our way, we have the assurance of this promise. It's like the foundation builders pour for the construction of a new house. With that foundation in place, the construction crew can proceed with confidence in building the structure. Similarly for those whom God fashions, His foundational promise of never leaving or forsaking us provides what we need to face any circumstance.

The winds may buffet us; they may even bend or knock us over. But the assurance of God's promise never ceases. No matter the situation, God is God. He has promised to stand with us during the good times and during the more challenging ones. Our victory is sure when we believe and trust that His promises are eternal. We endure; we press on because of His faithfulness. We praise Him for His seminal promise. Upon it we build a life of faithfulness to Him.

8

As it was in Jesus' time it is today. The disciple's walk is not for the fainthearted. *From this time many of his disciples turned back and no longer followed him.* (John 6:66) His invitation to them and to us was and is simple: "Follow me." Like many before us, we set out to fall in step with Him, but the way and His teachings are hard. Anxiety rears its head; uncertainty says, "Wait a minute." We hedge and equivocate. But this is no wishy-washy Savior to whom we have committed. With unwavering conviction He leads us onward toward the cross. Can we keep up? Will the walk to glory become too overwhelming? Will we yield to the temptation of the side roads that beckon us to stop for a while? Will pain and sorrow lead us off the trail He blazons? Will any of the challenges of the flesh obscure the road so that we lose sight of Him? For the fainthearted, the halfhearted, the answer sadly is, "Yes." But for those who understand surrender, who are transformed by His word into men and women of valor, who are determined no matter life's distractions to stay the course, the commitment to discipleship is sure. At the onset they discard any tendency toward faintheartedness into the first trash bin they pass. Mustering their faith through consistent prayer and persistent study of His word, they do not lose sight of Him. Nor do they forget the prize for which they strive by following Him. Like the apostle Paul, they *"press on toward the goal to win the prize for which God has called me heavenward in Christ Jesus."* (Philippians 3:4)

9

> *"So we make it our goal to please him… For we must all appear before the judgment seat of Christ that each one may receive what is due him for the things done while in the body."*
>
> 2 Corinthians 5:9–10

The apostle Paul understood an essential element of our faith that sometimes we gloss over, even ignore: We must live according to God's standards for one day we shall be held accountable. That truth of our faith is often not held to the light. Yes, we serve a gracious, loving and forgiving God who wants nothing more than our salvation. Of course He desires reconciliation with us; He made us in His image and likeness. Yet too often, especially in our contemporary culture, we relegate to the farthest regions of our faith that which Paul speaks to in his letter to the church at Corinth. Our faith requires that we both accept Jesus as Savior and that we live in accordance with God's will and purpose. The faithful accept that God's standards are the goals toward which we aspire. We accept that if we fail to meet those standards, we will be held accountable at the last judgment. We cannot gloss over this truth; it is fundamental. We cannot water down God's word. Only what we do to please the Master matters in the long run. If we stand before Him having accomplished His will and purposes for our lives, then we will hear those most cherished words spoken to us, "Well done, good and faithful servant."

10

"No temptation has overtaken you that is not common to man…"
I Corinthians 10:13

Let's see if we can get a firmer grasp of this concept of "temptation." Many believers fail to understand its broader meaning. Subsequently they tend to adopt an attitude of spiritual superiority when referencing it: "Oh, I'm seldom tempted toward carnal sin" or "I've never been tempted to do things like that." Scripture refutes this line of thinking. As Paul writes, there is no temptation we have not all faced at one time or another. Why? Because the concept of temptation implies more than its meaning of enticement toward wrong doing. As Paul writes, temptation also means trial, challenge and tribulation. This broader meaning helps us understand the close of the verse… "But when you are tempted, he will also provide the way of escape, that you may be able to endure it." We don't think of enticement toward evil or sin as something we endure. However we do understand the need to endure the trials and tribulations we face as part of the human condition. As we grasp that God's faithfulness is what helps and sustains us during these times, we are able to trust Him. We are able to hope in the eventual rescue He will provide as He leads us through the temptation we face.

11

They asked each other "Were not our hearts burning within us while he talked with us on the road and opened the Scriptures to us?"

Luke 24:32

When was the last time an encounter with the Lord caused your heart to burn within? Hopefully you can respond, "Why just this morning as I read my Bible, He set my soul on fire." Many who claim His name and call themselves Christians cannot respond in such fashion. Though they have publicly confessed Christ as Lord, their understanding of what that means has not yet penetrated. Their grasp of what and who they've committed to eludes them as it did the disciples walking along the road to Emmaus. They thought they knew, but when Jesus fulfilled in his crucifixion what had been foretold, they were baffled—*"but we had hoped that he was the one who was going to redeem Israel."* (Luke 24:21) Only after Jesus reiterated what the scriptures, beginning with Moses and the prophets, had said about Him did their hearts burn with understanding.

The same holds true for today's disciples. Our Savior's identity and the purpose for His coming can only be comprehended when we diligently study His word, when we allow the Holy Spirit to open the Scriptures to us. We encounter Jesus when we intentionally seek Him and the best place to find Him is the Bible. This Holy Word rescues us from the foolishness of the world; it opens our eyes and our heart to His salvation message. When we allow these divinely inspired words to penetrate the dullness of our minds, the Spirit lights a fire in our souls. Then empowered by that fire we can continue confidently upon the road He calls us to travel as His disciples.

12

> *Delight yourself in the Lord and he will give you the desires of your heart.*
>
> Psalm 37:4

Like most who have read this scripture countless times, I have understood it to mean one thing: God will give me what I want and desire. Period. Today however, I lingered over the words; not something I always do though I know I should. As I meditated, the essence of the scripture took on new meaning.

Clearly there is a condition placed upon the "giving." If I am to receive the desires of my heart, I must first delight myself in the Lord. To delight in God means to be fulfilled and satisfied by Him, not by things or persons or circumstances. To delight in God means to find joy in His presence and in His word. To delight in God means to surrender my will to His and to find solace and peace in so doing. Then, the God of all good gifts will give me the desires of my heart because only then will those desires reflect His intended plan for me. What the world offers will in no way measure up. We will only be satisfied with His desires for us and not our own. This deeper understanding of God's Word through reflective meditation is well worth the time it takes. Lingering over the word of God is a spiritual discipline worthy of cultivation.

13

Trust in the Lord with all your heart and lean not on your own understanding; in all your ways acknowledge him, and he will direct your path.

Proverbs 3:5–6

For several days my Old Testament readings were in Exodus (chapters 25–28) that describe in great detail the construction of the Ark of the Covenant, the priestly attire and other specifics of how worship was to be conducted by the Israelites on their journey to the Promised Land. Tedious reading for sure and I confess I did more skimming than actual reading. I felt these detailed chapters slowed the action of the story. I wanted to get back to the drama of how God victoriously led His people through a difficult period. Why, I wondered, did the writer of these biblical accounts devote so much time to this stuff? Frankly, it was boring!

Today as I lingered over the accounts, a new thought surfaced. What if God's purpose in spelling out the specifics of His instructions in such great detail was not just for these ancient people, but for us these many millennia later? Perhaps in so detailing these seemingly mundane undertakings in ark building and priestly garments, God was exercising His sovereignty in every aspect of their lives. With these specific details, He demonstrates to us He is interested and engaged in all facets of our lives too. Beyond the spiritual, He is to have imprint in the physical realm as well. He had a blueprint then; He has one now, designed to account for everything we will encounter from birth to eternity. We must be willing to follow His design and not one we create for ourselves.

Yes, the reading may be "boring." But these detailed accounts serve to remind us that even today, "God is in the details." And for that we are thankful.

14

And having been warned in a dream not to go back to Herod, they returned to their country by another route.
                                                    Matthew 2:12

The Magi had met Christ. And after this meeting they headed back from whence they had come by "another route." Is there meaning in this familiar passage for us today? Yes! As believers we too have met Christ. And the question is simple: Can we after such an encounter return to life as we knew it before, to the way we traveled before meeting Him? If we can and do, then an even more important question is, "Have we really met Him or was our encounter another superficial, shallow interaction common to the human experience? A real encounter, like the Magi's, demands change, an alternate route if you will, a new beginning, a conversion or transformation that causes us not to go back from whence we came; to things as they were before we met Him. If indeed we have "met" Him, we can't continue the same path.

Because we have met Him, we traverse a different road; the road that will lead us, if we stay the course, to His promise of eternal life.

15

Let us not grow weary in doing good, for at the proper time, we will reap a harvest if we do not give up.

Galatians 6:9

Sometimes this admonition of Paul's is the hardest thing to do. Try as we might to remain positive and upbeat when our goodwill gestures are met with indifference, ingratitude or received with a spirit of entitlement, we grow weary. Our spirits falter from the onslaught of these attitudes and actions. We wonder if our efforts are worth anything. In silence we suffer, wondering why God would have us continue to put forth the effort.

Perhaps when our spirits are their lowest, we need to reflect more upon the behavior of Christ and the apostles who followed Him. Neither gave up the good fight even though they may have had every reason to; considering the responses of many to whom they ministered. But the scriptures are filled with examples of them pressing onward with confidence. Paul's word to the church at Galatia assures us that God is not mocked and His word stands forever.(Galatians 6:7) We will reap what we sow. Knowing this and having the assurance that God is faithful to His word allows us not to give up, no matter the circumstances or the responses of others. The key is to remember we do what we do to glorify God.

16

"Whatever he saith unto you, do it."

John 2:5

Ever wonder how to master being in right relationship with the Lord? Here is your answer: Do whatever He tells you to do. Sounds simple, but any believer will confess the actual doing is the challenge. Not because we don't want to do what Jesus says to do, but because we often lack clarity. It's difficult to figure out how to live on one accord with Him. We stumble along, sometimes on the path He's ordained and sometimes not. We analyze the advantages and disadvantages of decisions and choices in every area of our lives. We hesitate; we equivocate.

We forget the best source for understanding what He requires is His word, the Bible. Therein are the answers that point to His expectations for us. The servants at the wedding feast in Cana got it right; when Jesus' mother said simply, *"Do whatever he says."* They did just that. As disciples of Jesus, that's what we are to do. If He said do it, we do. The Bible points the way; we follow. End result: right relationship with the Master!

17

A major challenge for disciples of Jesus Christ is remembering that only the Lord is worthy of our adulation and fascination. We live in an era of expose, of flash and bling, of the proverbial "15 minutes of fame" stretched ad nauseam by entertainment news programs, reality shows, talk shows, the ubiquitous YouTube and a multitude of other social media. It isn't easy to keep our eyes and minds on Jesus. We are easily distracted and being "stayed" on Him fades when images flash across the media, adorn magazine covers and the pages of pulp print. Like everyone else it seems, we get caught up in the glitz and glare. What are we to do? How do we live in the age of celebrity and still keep Christ in the forefront of our focus?

Sometimes it's the simple act of turning off the television, letting the computer sleep, ignoring the emails and messages on our smartphones and passing by the glossy call of print media. Choosing to begin the day in prayer and quiet time with God reading scripture and devotional materials helps a disciple to keep her priorities in order. Saturating oneself in the glory and grace of God allows little time for secular obsessions. The more of Christ we seek, the less appealing we find the world and its celebrities. Scripture tells us to *"Seek ye first the kingdom of God…"* When we do, we limit the power of the times to tempt us away from the only celebrity worthy of idolizing: Jesus Christ.

18

After we profess Christ as Lord and receive the salvation such a confession brings, we are the workers He uses to further kingdom building on earth. As His workers we are expected to advance His vision and purpose and to live so that His light shines in our attitudes and actions. All too often however, we yield to fear, to rejection, to pride, to secular pursuits and understandings. Such practices mimic those of Peter, one of Jesus' most trusted disciples. You recall his story. Following Jesus' arrest, and despite his prior declaration that he would never fall away or disown Jesus (Mark 14:29–31), he did just that when his allegiance was confronted. He failed the test of discipleship when he denied knowing Jesus.

Now it's easy to criticize Peter, to hold him up as an example of "talking the talk, but not walking the walk." With biblical hindsight we can proclaim that had we spent three years walking alongside and working with Jesus, we would most certainly have "had His back" when He was arrested. We proclaim as much even as we do today the same thing Peter did then. "How so?" Glad you asked. Each time we turn away from someone in need, we deny Jesus. Each time we speak hurtful words or engage in idle gossip, we deny Jesus. Each time we give priority to our agendas and schedules instead of allowing God to direct us, we deny Jesus. Each time we fail to offer a word of hope, of encouragement, or to reach out to the least, the last, the lost, we deny Jesus. A rude word or action denies Jesus. A misuse of resources denies Jesus. A refusal to serve in kingdom building denies Jesus. A reluctance to witness to God's goodness denies Jesus. We all have the potential to be "Peter" in the courtyard and deny the Master. Our hope and prayer each day is that we will not be fearful or weak as Jesus' fellow workers; but will stand courageously at every turn to proclaim Him by our actions in word and deed.

19

Jesus said to his disciples, "I tell you the truth, if you have faith as small as a mustard seed, you can say to this mountain, 'Move from here to there' and it will move. Nothing will be impossible for you."

Matthew 17:20–21

A pastor friend of mine once told us that we need "a faith that out performs your problems." It's a briefer version to me of Jesus' response to His followers when they asked why they had been unable to drive out a demon spirit. We contemporary disciples are often like them. We try but are unable to "drive out" those things that separate us from the Lord. We forget the power we possess when we accept Jesus. We need what the pastor proclaimed. Ponder Jesus' words again in the scripture above. Literal Mountain moving seems impossible. But Jesus says that with faith, we can do it. Nothing he tells the disciples will be impossible if their faith is as it should be.

We probably aren't concerned with moving Mt Rainer to another location, but all of us have some kind of "mountain" that needs to be moved—the mountain of fear that prevents us from moving forward; the mountain of pain and grief that keeps us bogged down in sorrow; the mountain of sin that obscures the forgiveness of God; the mountain of anxiety and worry that blocks abundant living in Christ. Jesus said it over two thousand years ago and my pastor restated it in his sermon. Sufficient faith conquers problems. Disciples must decide to allow that kernel of faith to empower them to overcome what appears impossible. Within that small seed of faith rests the power to perform in spite of circumstances. With its actualization, God's omnipotence is realized.

20

> *... Now Joseph was a disciple of Jesus, but secretly because he feared the Jews.*
>
> John 19:38

This verse of scripture captures an exceedingly sad moment in the crucifixion and burial of Christ. A man identified as Joseph of Arimathea secures permission from Pilate to claim the body of Jesus. Though scripture tells us he was one of Jesus' disciples, apparently no one else at the time knew this little tidbit. Joseph of Arimathea hid his faith. He lived in fear of exposure; he was willing to embrace Jesus' teachings out of the public eye, but he could not stand in the light of Christ openly. Many such "Josephs" live today, accepting Jesus within the cloistered walls of the faith community, but hiding their faith convictions beyond them. For perhaps the same reasons as Joseph of Arimathea, they fear ridicule in the workplace; they fear that in their ascent on whatever ladders they climb, their secret will be revealed. How sad that the biblical Joseph was not brave enough before Jesus' death to live his faith in the open like the other disciples. We may laud his gesture of goodwill at the end; he did prepare the body for proper burial. But we can only speculate as to his potential influence as a wealthy, influential supporter during Jesus' ministry had he not been a secret disciple. Today we do well to remember this Joseph. We who profess Christianity are called to proclaim our faith openly, without hesitation and certainly without fear. Secular success has no reward great enough to lure us into anonymity in our relationship with Jesus. Secret discipleship is no discipleship at all.

21

> *Jesus looked at him and loved him. "One thing you lack," he said. "Go sell everything you have and give to the poor, and you will have treasure in heaven. Then come, follow me." At this the man's face fell. He went away sad because he had great wealth.*
>
> Mark 10:21–22

Ever wonder why Jesus spoke as He did to the man who eagerly sought to know what he must do to get to heaven? He was obedient to the law, and scripture says that Jesus "loved him." His obedience and enthusiasm for Jesus would seem just the characteristics to make him a worthy disciple. Add to those features his apparent wealth and the resources for kingdom building they would provide and wonderment turns to puzzlement. Why doesn't Jesus snatch up this young man right then! He could have directed the use of the man's possessions in ways that would not comprise His message.

Our answer comes in two parts. First, Jesus needed nothing the man thought he owned; what he had came from God in the first place. He only needed the man to recognize that. Secondly, we look at the man's reaction to Jesus' answer. His fallen countenance and sadness of spirit suggest that the price of salvation was too high. Why? Because the value he places on his possessions was greater than the value he gave to the potential inheritance of eternal life. Jesus knew that. Though the man was probably what we would call a "good person," someone who abided by the tenets of the law, he lacked the one thing Jesus seeks in any of us who claim His name: total abandonment and submission to Him alone. What we own; our possessions, our status, nothing has significance in the light of

Jesus' call and in the path leading to eternal life. Everything we are and have must submit to Him. That notion was just too hard for the would-be disciple. He could not recognize the source of his stuff, nor could he let go of it. The lesson for us is clear. Following Jesus means total surrender.

22

"Oh the joy of meeting Jesus." This song lyric speaks of that appointed time in the future when we get to heaven. I suggest that the glory and joy of meeting Jesus is possible for us right now as we journey on that road to heaven! How so? Think for a moment. Every time we open God's Word and read the writings He inspired, the opportunity to joyfully encounter Jesus is ours. The Bible gives us Jesus' words, His teachings for living. That knowledge brings joy each time we follow it as an example of how to live on earth anticipating living one day with the Lord. What emotion can such consideration bring except joy! Scripture tells us to "rejoice in the Lord always;" not at some future time, but right now. Complete joy will be our overwhelming response when we finally stand before the Master, but we don't have to wait until then. We have a chance each day to know the joy of the Lord. We greet Him in joy each morning He awakens us from sleep. Throughout the day we feel the joy of His presence and when we lay our heads down for another night's rest, we do so with joy that He has been faithful once again. Maybe the lyrics ought to be, "Oh the joy of meeting Jesus every single day!"

23

Remember the words of Isaiah the prophet, "Here I am. Send me." (Isaiah 6:8–9) Often we refer to them when we speak of responding to God's call to be servants in His kingdom. We aspire to the same level of willing servanthood that the Prophet's response implied. God asked, *"Whom shall I send? Who will go for us?"* Without hesitation, Isaiah uttered his famous words. It is worth our reflection to note what happened prior to this exchange of call and response that speaks to the heart of what it means to serve God. Isaiah first had to confess his unworthiness, his sin, and then be absolved of that sin by the live coals from God's altar that were placed on his lips. As an imminent prophet he had to be cleansed from his unrighteousness before he could in purity do the work God commissioned him to do (Isaiah 6:5–7)

Likewise for us today. True servanthood demands more than just a simple, "I'll do it." The kind of service God seeks from His followers will require confession of sin and total submission of our will to His purposes. Such prerequisites are not easy; often they require pain and anguish; those live coals surely burned Isaiah's lips! Understandably, seeking to be God's servant will take us through an atonement process to burn away what stands as an obstacle to our service. Before God uses us, He refines us so that the service we render reflects His glory and not ours.

24

I read the phrase "suffering the will of God" in a devotional and immediately thought: God's will is not something believers suffer, rather the opposite. God's will is something in which we rejoice! There are those who hold the notion that doing the Lord's will is something that must be endured, as one endures suffering. They believe that through "suffering" His will our reward comes. To me such an attitude is too "hang dog, too whinny, too woe is me." On the contrary, God's will should be embraced with enthusiasm. When we are in His will, we can echo the words of the psalmist, *"The Lord has done great things for us and we are glad."* (Psalm 126:3)

His will for us is perfect no matter how it might appear to be to the human eye or to human understanding. Even when it seems His will allows trials and tribulations, we do not yield to a spirit of defeat or joylessness. Amidst the suffering, we remember Jesus whose suffering for us was far greater than anything we endure. With that remembrance, our attitude is different; we look upon our circumstance not as suffering God's will, but as yielding to God's will. And when we can yield, when we achieve that level of surrender, His will is not odious; rather it becomes something we embrace with assurance that He will ride the wave with us. No matter how high the torrent of water reaches, we will in His time emerge victorious, according to His will.

25

What image of Christ do others see when they look at us? As Christians we must be sure the image we project confirms the name we proclaim. Our faces, the tone of our expressions, our actions all portray who we are. When we think of our public persona, we must be careful that what we think we portray is what others see. When you're in a hurry in the grocery store and the person in front of you at the checkout counter is fumbling to pay for the purchases or even more frustrating deciding what items to put back, what look adorns your face? Impatience? Eyes rolling upward? Lips drawn tightly? What about when the freeway backs up making you late for the doctor's appointment. What does your expression say to the driver in the car next to you? Are you leaning fruitlessly on the horn, adding to the frustration of the other drivers? When the kids in the booth nearest you in the restaurant are loud and whinny and the parents seem oblivious to the disturbance they are causing, what does the look on your face proclaim? Annoyance? And what does your expression reveal when you're in a work meeting and the boss takes credit for your ideas? Can your colleagues detect your feelings of disbelief and disgust?

In any of these situations, the natural response is typically to show impatience, annoyance, anger, indignation. But disciples of Jesus are called to a higher standard. We are those who belong to the Savior; by His grace we have crucified these tendencies that give rise to these reactions. We have mastered, and continue to master when we fall short, the fruit of the spirit that the Apostle Paul tells us to put on: love, patience, kindness, gentleness, joy, peace and self-control.

26

God doesn't want to manifest Himself to us, but in us. *"See to it then, that the light within you is not darkness."* (Luke 11:35) We get hung up on the idea of waiting for the Lord to show up, to reveal Himself to us in our circumstance. God in the meantime is trying to reveal Himself in us, in our thoughts, our words and our deeds as we live in the circumstance. *"But the seed on good soil stands for those with a noble and good heart, who hear the word, retain it, and by preserving produce a crop."* (Luke 8:15) What we tend to forget is that the manifestation of Himself to us is just one side of the coin. If we only have manifestations we can easily get the "big head" or develop a superiority complex because we think we've had an experience with the Lord no one else has had. "Oh, the Lord has really showed up in my situation. Let me tell you what He did." All the attention is on us in this circumstance.

The other side of the coin which shifts the focus from us to God occurs when His spirit is glorified by its manifestation in us. When the Spirit of the Lord manifests itself in us, often there is no need tell anyone anything. The light of His spirit shines so brightly in our countenance, our words and our deeds that others know it's the Lord having His way in our circumstance. I believe that this is what Jesus meant when He spoke about the lamp on a stand: *"No one lights a lamp and puts it in a jar or puts it under a bed. Instead, he puts it on a stand, so that those who come in can see the light."* (Luke 8:16) As the Apostle Paul so eloquently expresses, Jesus Himself is the light. He not only wants to reveal Himself to us, but as importantly to manifest Himself in us. For it is when others see the light of Christ in us that they are most likely to want that light for themselves. It's not what we proclaim about the light of Christ that matters, but whether the light we proclaim lives in and is visible in us.

27

To whom will you liken me and make me equal, and compare me, as though we were alike? Those who lavish gold from the purse, and weigh out silver in the scales—they have a goldsmith, who makes it into a god; then they fall down and worship! They lift it to their shoulders, they carry it; they set it in its place, shout to it, it does not answer or save anyone from trouble.

Isaiah 46:5–70

As I reflected upon these words of the prophet Isaiah, I thought how misguided were these people about whom he spoke. How could they worship gold and silver idols or think them capable of meeting their needs? Yet, I thought, we are not all that different; even with our knowledge of what happened to the people as they experienced defeat and exile and alienation from God. How great is our tendency to equate God with the gods of our times and in so doing alienate ourselves from Him? Though we know there is none like Him, that He alone is omnipotent, we nonetheless are quick to elevate the gods of our times to places of importance.

Think for a moment. We invest tremendous time, effort and resources acquiring the very things that have the dangerous potential to separate us from God. On our way to success and prosperity, we elevate these secular acquisitions to godlike status. High indeed are the banners we carry proclaiming what we have accomplished in the world's eyes. When are we most likely to confess that nothing in the secular realm has any lasting power? When those very symbols of power and might stand silent as the winds of challenge and adversity blow our way. Then we admit the money, the gold card, the mansion, the job, the influence have little or no power to save us. Then we admit only God almighty is our Savior. Then we proclaim He alone is worthy of our worship as He alone delivers us from peril and destruction. Hallelujah to the one and only God!

28

Wait for the Lord; be strong and take heart and wait for the Lord.

Psalm 27:14

Often the hardest thing for believers to master is this waiting on God. We know the scripture that tells us to, but still when it comes down to the doing, we struggle. Issues press; we feel powerless. We want action now! Perhaps we struggle with the concept of waiting because it doesn't come naturally. In early childhood when our parent said, "Wait a minute," that only served to intensify our whining and demanding. Even teens and young adults consider "waiting" a novel concept; they want what they desire now and not in some vague point in the future.

But disciples of Jesus Christ have moved beyond these stages of instant gratification and spiritual immaturity. They understand they are called to live in a way that demonstrates how to "wait on the Lord." Though it may be challenging, disciples do not yield to the pressure to take matters into their own hands. Only with God's direction do they move forward. They understand that for those who can wait patiently, God is faithful to point the way. True, Gods' resolution of an issue or circumstance may be different than wanted or expected. But disciples accept that God knows best. His thoughts and mind are so far superior to ours that we refuse to question His responses or His deliverance plan. Disciples ascribe to the words of David when he writes, *"I waited patiently for the Lord, he turned to me and heard my cry."* (Psalm 40:1)

29

As I read a devotional piece, I am always on the alert for an idea, sentence or phrase that speaks directly to my heart and deepens my faith. I found it today in a closing sentence by Erwin Lutzer: "Nothing will make us closer to God than being forced to walk in unfamiliar territory." Think about it. When we're moving along with little or no tears in our life's tapestry, when we operate almost on automatic pilot day in and day out, we don't feel much need for more than a cursory relationship with God—going to church occasionally, reading the Bible sporadically, praying perfunctorily—are enough of a commitment. But God has His ways. Recall the Israelites, forced to walk for 40 years in unfamiliar territory totally dependent upon God. Eventually they grew to understand the relationship God required of them in the strange places they found themselves. God demanded obedience to His will and purposes for their lives. He hasn't changed.

Today, we most often draw closer to Him only after He has allowed us to wander in unfamiliar territory—the land of death of a loved one, the island of illness, the lagoon of lost employment, the sea of separation or divorce, the chasm of a child's rebellion, the barrier of betrayal. As we trudge about in these strange places, we may seek solace at first from sources other than God; our own versions of the golden calf, false idols that initially dull the pain for a moment, but ultimately leave us feeling even more afraid and alone. It is usually at this point in the journey that we finally turn to the Savior. We seek Him, His comfort and peace as we surrender our will to His. And we say as did Joshua to the Israelites, *"But for me and my house, we will serve the Lord."* (Joshua 24:14–15)

30

> *"Brothers, we do not want you to be ignorant about those who fall asleep, or to grieve like the rest of men who have no hope."*
> I Thessalonians 4:13

A definitive mark of our faith witness is our response to death, especially the death of a loved one. Having walked in the valley myself I know the depth of sorrow that shrouds the way. What I discovered however was that my faith in God and belief in Jesus' resurrection from death as Scripture teaches kept me from losing hope. Amidst the pain and numbness of death's reality, that spark of hope burned sufficiently to sustain my spirit. I discovered that even as we move through "the valley of the shadow of death," God manifests His presence in unexpected ways.

Seeking personal comfort at a grief support group meeting, I shared my story with those gathered there. Ironically, my testimony of God's faithfulness during the season of my sorrow gave the comfort I came seeking to others in the group. His word tells us that He is strong in our weakness. In this instance He revealed that strength by using my grief experience to comfort and empower others.

In the midst of our circumstances, we can trust Him to further His purposes for our lives. When we accept this truth of our faith, then we do not grieve like unbelievers. Yes, we feel sorrow and pain at such times, but our faith and trust in God's everlasting word keeps us moving toward healing and restoration. When death's arrow finds it mark, we remember that Jesus has conquered death and those of us who believe in Him will do likewise.

31

See the Lord's hand is not too short to save, nor his ear too dull to hear. Rather, your iniquities have been barriers between you and God, and your sins have hidden his face from you so that he does not hear.

Isaiah 59:1–2

I was struck by the common sense of these words written by the prophet Isaiah. Of course we know of God's omnipotence and His omniscience. He alone defines what it means to be mighty and all knowing. When we turn to Him for relief from adversity, we do so in confidence. Yet there are times when the relief we seek does not come. We are confused; we know He hears us and His arm of mercy can surely reach us, but nothing happens. In this passage Isaiah gives us a reasonable answer why. Our transgressions are blocking our blessings. Obviously it is worthwhile before the next life experiences send you to your knees in supplication to examine yourself beforehand. Are you in right relationship with the Lord? Are there sins that remain unconfessed and block His intervention? Common sense tells us it is ridiculous to go to God seeking His divine touch without having asked for forgiveness.

Our souls must be right with the Savior if we expect His touch and answered prayer. He tells us clearly that when His word abides in us and we abide in Him (i.e. we are obedient to His will), we can ask whatever we wish and He will hear us. (John 15:7)

32

Is it just me or does anyone else think it's odd that an officiating pastor would ask the congregants gathered to witness a religious wedding ceremony, if it would okay for him to offer a prayer? A friend who attended the wedding shared the highlights, including the reverend's comment. She noted that as the ceremony drew to a close, the minister said, "If anyone doesn't mind, I'd like to offer a prayer." It wasn't until the day after this conversation that the minister's comment stirred my thinking. Why, I wondered, would a man who professes God and serves as a chaplain think he had to ask for permission to pray? Even as I suspect the chapel itself is nondenominational, for the couple who chose it rather than a civil venue, prayer offered by the chaplain would be the norm.

I conclude that the officiant's request is a manifestation of how interwoven the church and the secular have become. Not wanting to offend anyone present who just might not believe in prayer, he chose to be "politically correct," to blur the line between the sacred and the secular by the accommodation of getting permission first. Suppose someone had objected to prayer? Imagine the shock at that moment. What would the bride and groom have done? More importantly, what response would the minister have given? Would he have bowed to that voice of dissent to keep peace? Our hope is that those who serve God in leadership roles will never yield to cultural norms, but stand firm in their faith at all times, boldly witnessing to it as the Lord's shepherds on earth. Shame on said pastor for his failure to do so on this occasion.

33

Is anyone else like me when it comes to prayer? I am always faithful to begin each day in communion with God in prayer. In fact, getting on my knees to pray is my first act of the morning. It's not hard then. The miracle of opening my eyes to another day elicits a prayerful posture almost automatically. The promise of a new day is joyous and the need to express thanksgiving and gratitude bursts forth with little effort. And staying in prayer throughout the day is not much of a struggle either. How easily prayerful expressions spill from my lips as I perceive mundane events as directly touched by the Master's hand. "Thank you, Jesus." "Praise the Lord." "Walk with me now, Lord." "Go with me Father into this den of lions." Talking to God as I move from one thing to another is effortless.

My struggle, and maybe yours too if you're anything like me, is reaching the end of the day and not being as disciplined in prayer as I was in the morning and throughout the day. So much has gone on through the course of those fourteen or fifteen hours that by the time I turn off the television or put down my book or smartphone, I rush through a prayer of thanksgiving and often fall asleep in the midst of it. Even as I drift off, I feel convicted that I have shortchanged the Savior, the One who blessed me throughout the day. I always promise to do better the next evening, forgetting that only God knows if a next evening is even on the drawing board for me. This reads more like a confession than a devotional, but I offer it anyway. The disciple's cross is not easy; it's not supposed to be. Vigilance in all things is required to be ready to meet the Lord. Maybe my struggle in this area of my faith journey will inspire someone else to not give up, to press on toward the prize that awaits the faithful. We serve a gracious, forgiving God who loves us in spite of our muttered, mumbled, drifting evening prayers.

Addendum: Since I wrote this sometime ago, I'm happy to report that I'm getting better. My evening prayers are purposeful and offered more times than not before I fall asleep!

34

When one of my granddaughters was in second grade her curriculum included the study of verb tenses. Each day she had to identify the tense of a verb by its action in a sentence. Her choices were past, present and future. Someone struggling to understand who God is might gain clarity from these parts of speech properties of an action verb. God has acted in the past; He acts in the present and He will act in the future. In biblical history and in our own history, God acted (past) to bring about His purposes. In my granddaughter's lessons, the past action verb is often tagged with the letters, "ed." They signal to her that the action has already occurred. The Bible itself is the composite "ed" of God's actions. It tells us what He has already done in the world and for those who believe and follow Him. Reading of His past actions helps us know Him as our divine Sustainer and Redeemer.

Our understanding of what He has done allows us to grasp what He is doing now (present) to foster His purposes for all of creation. God is a present force swirling in and through the realities of living. As scripture tells us, "… *the word of God is living and active…*" (Hebrews 4:12) And since no time parameters limit the word of the Lord, we can be confident of its reality in the future; that time that stretches before us until the day of Christ's "Second Coming." As we wait for that day, God orchestrates the future as surely as He has the past and is currently doing in the present. He is our past tense, our present tense, and our future tense; the divine personification of each.

35

The aim in life for the believer is to live God's will and not our own. "We make it our aim…to be well pleasing to him."
2 Corinthians 5:9

Why is that so hard to do? I mean, we want to live in His will; we pray to Him to live in His will; we accept that our confession of Him as our Lord and Savior means we agree to live in His will. But our reality is that we do not. Instead we live in our own will and attempt to fashion God's will in and around ours.

Maybe this concept of "living in God's will" is difficult because our understanding of what that means is murky. After all, we go to church on Sundays; we do a little volunteer work; as we are able we give our offerings; we are typically loving of family and friends and neighbor; we donate to the less fortunate. Aren't we in His will when we do all this? Well, perhaps we are; but even those who may not share our faith convictions do most of those same things. What distinguishes us? What sets us apart as a people of faith who live God's will and not our own?

It is the mark of those who understand that one day *"We must all appear before the judgment seat of Christ, that each one may receive what is due him for the things done while in the body, whether good or bad."* (2 Corinthians 5:10) The murkiness recedes when we grasp that we will be held accountable and judged by what we have done. Only the things done that were in God's purposes will matter. Perhaps then, the question isn't "Why is it so hard? But rather "How can I be sure this is God's will and not my own?" The answer is now easier to come by. God's will for us is laid out clearly in His word to us. If we approach the Bible as our blueprint for living, then abiding in His will is less of a challenge. The difficulty—the why is it so hard—arises when we turn from the resource He provides and choose our own way.

36

However, as it is written: "No eye has seen, no ear has heard, no mind has conceived what God has prepared for those who love him."
I Corinthians 2:9

The words of an old song came to mind as I read this scripture: "The best is yet to come." They capture precisely Paul's message to the believers at the church in Corinth to whom he wrote this epistle. For us today, it is important to remember the truth of this lyrical sentiment and the gospel's proclamation. For those of us who truly love the Lord, the best He has to offer is yet to be revealed.

Oh, many think they've reached the pinnacle of success in their professional, personal and even spiritual lives. For them their ascent to the mountaintop in these areas is proof sufficient that they have achieved the best life has to offer. But those who understand the omnipotence of God comprehend that He is more than what the eye sees in the natural. In fact, He is so awesome that our minds cannot fathom His greatness. If we think of the world's best in any category, it is diminished when placed against what the Lord has and wants to offer the faithful. The lesson of this scripture is an appreciation of what a mighty God we serve. No matter our current circumstances as we remain true to Him, He will meet us not just at our points of need, but over and beyond. *"Now to him who is able to do immeasurably more than all we ask or imagine..."* (Ephesians 3:20)

37

Jesus was a model teacher, exemplary in fact. Today we would select Him "Teacher of the Year" every year! He knew the most effective teaching strategy: modeling the desired outcome of the lesson. One of the most important goals of His divine lesson plan was to develop in His students the fruit of the Spirit: love, joy, peace, patience, kindness, goodness, faithfulness, gentleness and self-control (See Galatians 5:22–23) He understood the best way to do that was by exemplifying those attributes of the Spirit in His living. So He did. Day in and day out, Jesus in His portable classroom taught what the fruit of God's Spirit looked like, talked like and acted like. Sufficient numbers of pupils got it! They followed His "guided practice" until eventually they mastered the lesson objective. Their lives were transformed and they were themselves able to model the lesson for other.

We who profess Christ today are in the same sense His students, striving to master His lesson plan objectives. We know His goal is still for us to exemplify the fruit of the Spirit in word, thought and deed. Each day we seek to follow His instructions and apply the lesson goal in our living. Anything less dishonors the eternal "Teacher of the Ages" and places our success as His students at risk.

38

> *"My people come to you, as they usually do, and sit before you to listen to your words, but they do not put them into practice. With mouths they express devotion... Indeed to them you are nothing more than one who sings love songs with a beautiful voice and plays an instrument well, for they hear your words but do not put them into practice."*
>
> Ezekiel 33:31–32

As I read these verses I thought of worship service in churches today. I think we are often like those exiled Israelites who would gather to hear God's word spoken through the prophet Ezekiel. They came to be entertained rather than enlightened as evidenced by their failure to "do" God's word after they heard it. Though we would deny it, many of us go to church to be entertained. The nature of contemporary worship lends itself to that as aspects of the service often prompt applause, even standing ovations. The choir's soaring renditions, the musicians' mastery of the organ, the keyboard, the drums and other instruments; even the preached Word itself—all are received with hand clapping, our universal sign of approval and admiration. Why, I have on occasion heard tepid applause following a fervent prayer. And though I join in applause at various time during a service, in the back of my mind I'm wondering what exactly am I applauding? The "performance" of the worship prompters or what? Does applause laud the performer as it often appears to, or is it an expression of my intent to be obedient to God's call on my life?

It's easy to fall into the mindset of our biblical ancestors referenced in the scripture above. Worship is intended to draw us closer to God, to a surrendered life to Him and obedience to His word. If our applause is a sign that we are saying "Yes" to Him and intend to turn away from sin, then applauding is justified. But if we are standing to applaud the individuals who prompt the service, then we're missing the point of worship. We attend church for inspiration and instruction, to be reminded of how to live righteously and to put this knowledge into practice each day. We are not there to be entertained.

39

> *"Here I am! I stand at the door and knock. If anyone hears my voice and opens the door, I will come in and eat with him, and he with me."*
>
> Revelation 3:20

Maybe our Christian walk would be easier if Jesus adopted the "B and E" modus operandi. If instead of waiting outside the door of our hearts, He just broke down the door and entered, then we'd have no choice except surrender. Like those who are victims of breaking and entering in the physical domain, we would give up in recognition of a power greater than ours and do whatever He wanted us to do.

But that's not Jesus' style, is it? We serve a courteous God. If you want a model of graciousness, look no farther. Jesus is no barbarian. With divine politeness, He knocks and waits for us to say, "Come in." The choice to open the door is ours to make. He announces Himself, but doesn't force Himself upon us. If we open the door, He comes in; if we don't, He doesn't and won't. Yes, we might wish that He didn't give us such freedom of choice. In some ways, it's easier to be manipulated; such a model requires little conscious or consciousness.

We serve a God who created us and gave us a heart and a mind. When we open the door of our heart to His love and accept His entrance into our lives, we take on the "mind of Christ." And such a mind recognizes that though God is omnipotent, He is not oppressive. The decision to follow Him is always ours to declare.

40

"...so is my word that goes out from my mouth; It will not return to me empty, but will accomplish what I desire and achieve the purpose for which I sent it."

Isaiah 55:11

Think for a moment what these words of God spoken by His prophet Isaiah mean for us who profess Christ as our Lord and Savior. God's word, the Bible, contains many commands and His directions for righteous living. Nothing contained in the holy document is frivolous. Always there is a word from the Lord; and that word always has a purpose. Our Bible is for us what a playbook is for the athlete. We each use our playbook to guide and instruct us toward a defined purpose. And just as the coach watches to see if his players will execute the plays as they are outlined to achieve the victory the team seeks, God watches us. Our playbook, the Bible, contains all the procedures we need to live a victorious life of faith.

41

Then Nebuchadnezzar was furious with Shadrach, Meshach and Abednego, and his attitude toward them changed.

Daniel 3:19

Most believers who endeavor to live their faith understand what it means to have attitudes toward them change. As did these three friends of Daniel, we may for a time enjoy the favor and benefits that come with being held in high esteem within our family circle, community or workplace. But few manage the journey to glory without running into roadblocks, detours or dead ends. Often these circumstances confront us when we are forced to make choices that challenge those in authority or whose beliefs differ from ours.

We remember the story of the young Jewish exiles whose exceptional talents had so impressed the king that he had given them authority to rule several of his provinces. Life was good until jealous "haters" called to the king's attention the fact that the three men defied his royal order for everyone to bow to a golden image. Angered by such flagrant disobedience, the king issued a "do it or else" command. In what was clearly a life or death moment, the young men stood firm in their faith and refused. They declared openly that God could save them, and even if He did not, they would not sin against Him by bowing to an idol. Offended by their integrity and faithfulness to their God, the king's attitude towards them changed.

Often when we face those decision making moments that test our faith commitment, we should not be surprised that others change their attitudes toward us. Such attitude changing goes with the territory. Jesus told us we could not serve two masters, the world and God. Conflict between the two is unavoidable. And attitudes toward you that were positive, when conflict was dormant, can easily flip to negative. A believer whose faith is firmly rooted will not deny it when circumstances change. Regardless of potential consequences, the faithful refuse to compromise their beliefs to submit to anything that hinders their progress toward eternity with the Lord.

42

As we discussed the lesson in a Bible study class, one of our pastors who facilitated the course asked the question, "What if God was sitting next to you right now?" "No!" someone declared loudly. The class broke into spontaneous laughter. "He is, you know," the pastor continued as the laughter died down. "We say He's omnipresent, right? So that means He's right here now in our midst." That incident surfaced one morning as I quietly engaged in my devotional time. God is here, I thought. I imagined Him resting on the loveseat opposite me waiting for me to finish my reading and reflective journaling. He would be like that; not intrusive or demanding, just patiently waiting for me to center my attention upon Him.

Suddenly I realized that no matter what's going on in my life, that's exactly what God is doing; waiting for me to cast aside everything that keeps me from what ought to be my primary focus: Him alone. How easily we get caught up in the "doing" of our faith and forget that what God desires first and foremost is for us to seek His face. To know the Lord intimately is a deliberate pursuit, one that calls us to spend quiet quality time in His presence, in communion with Him, drawing upon His strength and wisdom. Once filled with His spirit, we are equipped to carry out His plans and fulfill His purposes. Then when someone asks, "Suppose God was sitting now right next to you?" Instead of a panicky "No," our response would be a calm, "Oh yes, I know He is. He's my constant companion no matter where I am."

43

"My prayer is not for them alone; I pray also for those who will believe in me through their message, that all of them may be one, Father, just as you are in me and I am in you. May they also be in us so that the world may believe that you have sent me."
John 17:20–21

As Jesus concluded His last teachings to the disciples before His arrest and crucifixion, He ended His words of guidance and wisdom with prayer. He prayed for himself, for the disciples present with Him and finally for "those who will believe." That's us!! Isn't it awe inspiring to know that over two thousand years ago, Jesus Himself prayed for us! The Son of God incarnate paused before His ultimate sacrifice on the cross and resurrection from the tomb to pray for believers yet to be born. When the reality of that moment strikes home, we are stopped in our tracks. We have known and lived in the prayers of our fore parents, mothers and fathers and Christian friends and family. But none of these prayers raise the "wow" factor as a prayer from Jesus' own lips.

Once we internalize it, we are astonished at the implication of the Scripture. God and likewise His Son, Jesus knew that one day you and I would profess our faith in Him. Jesus prayed that we would achieve unity with all believers and with Him and God the Father. He prayed for this unity so that through it the world would know with certainty that God sent Jesus from Heaven into the world. Knowing that before we were the proverbial "twinkle in our father's eyes," Jesus prayed for us that we might be ongoing witnesses to the greatest truth ever written or told: *For God so loved the world that he gave his one whoever believes in him shall not perish but have eternal life.* (John 3:16)

44

A man of many companions may come to ruin, but there is a friend who sticks closer than a brother.
Proverbs 18:24

Whenever this familiar proverb is offered as comfort or encouragement, the reference is usually made that Jesus is that "friend who sticks closer than a brother." Like most Christians I easily accept this reality because Jesus of course offers us true friendship, unconditional love and eternal salvation. When my husband died suddenly some years ago, the words of the proverb sprang to life during the days and weeks that followed. My "coming to ruin" was the actual loss of my soulmate of more than 35 years with no forewarning of the impending disaster. The friend who stuck closer than a brother was indeed the Lord. In those first moments and those first days, it was the comforting presence of the Holy Spirit that kept me sane, putting one foot in front of the other to do what needed to be done. I understand that God was even more of a friend than the words of the proverb suggest. He not only stayed by my side Himself, He provided the means for my family and sister friends to come to care for me as well.

These loved ones were the tangible extensions of God's grace and mercy during my walk in death's valley. To know and feel the Lord's comforting assurance during such times is the ultimate blessing. Second unto it is His provision for family and friends who stick close until the "ruin" is manageable.

45

> *Again the Israelites did evil in the eyes of the Lord, and for seven years he gave them into the hands of the Midianites...Midian so impoverished the Israelites that they cried out to the Lord for help. When the Israelites cried to the Lord because of Midian he sent them a prophet who said, "This is what the Lord, the God Israel, says: 'I brought you up out of Egypt... I said to you, I am the Lord you God; do not worship the gods of the Amorites, in whose land you live. But you have not listened to me."... When the angel of the Lord appeared to Gideon he said, "The Lord is with mighty warrior." "But sir," Gideon replied, "If the Lord is with us, why has all this happened to us? ...But now the Lord has abandoned us and put us into the hand of Midian."*
>
> Judges 6:1–13

This story of a lesser known servant of the Lord's during Israel's on again-off again relationship with God is worthy of attention.

Gideon's response to the angel reminds me of how we respond to God when we are in the midst of adverse circumstances caused by disobedience. Forced to thresh his wheat in a winepress to avoid detection by the Midianites, Gideon in essence asks, "If God is with us, then why are we suffering, hiding in caves and mountain clefts in order to survive?" How often have you or someone you know voiced the same questions; "Lord, if You are faithful, then why am I in the throes of my current crisis? Why aren't You coming to my rescue?" I think we like Gideon forget that often times we are responsible for the onslaught of our adversities. We forget God's mercy and grace and turn again to lifestyles that defy His will and purposes. We fail to be obedient and our disobedience leads to sin which leads to difficult circumstances. As our suffering intensifies we cry out to God for help.

The lesson for us as we reflect upon this cycle of "sin-crisis-cry for help-forgiveness-deliverance-sin again" is we might avoid the suffering that sin inevitably produces if we would just be obedient to God's word. Not that I am suggesting we will encounter no problems by faithful living, but we might avoid the suffering we bring on ourselves when we deliberately disobey God.

46

I watched Mel Gibson's *Passion of the Christ* again over the weekend. No matter how many times you watch it, it's impossible to view this contemporary cinematic expression of Jesus' betrayal, arrest, trial and crucifixion without dread and tears. We read the account in our Bibles, but when it's enacted in living color, the gruesome reality of Jesus' pain and suffering can't be filtered. I understand the film maker probably took some dramatic license in the portrayal, but what we see is probably very close to the truth of what the priests, soldiers and bystanders actually did to Him. We wonder as we watch how on earth He endured it.

Because Jesus was both human and divine, we might say, "Well, His divinity gave Him superhuman strength and endurance. He was immune to the pain because of that." That line of thought may have validity, but I think there's another answer; one that gives us the similar strength to face our trials as Jesus faced His. Jesus as Son of Man was able to endure the suffering and the pain of passion because He had lived during His ministry preparing for it. His preparation was simple; He often withdrew to pray. *"But Jesus often withdrew to lonely places to pray."* (Luke 5:16) I believe that Jesus' discipline of unceasing prayer enabled Him to suffer the anguish of His ultimate sacrifice. Fervent prayer brings closer communion with God the Father. Fervent prayer allows the Holy Spirit to give comfort and assurance. Fervent prayer drives out fear and replaces it with peace. Fervent prayer evokes joy. Fervent prayer supplies the physical, emotional and spiritual strength we need to endure every tribulation, every crisis. And when our custom has been to pray continually, whether the day is sunny and bright or dark and stormy, we find our prayer reservoir is filled to the brim, running over even. It is when this state of our souls is supported by an unrelenting prayer life that we can withstand anything. We can like Jesus suffer the losses, pains and devastations and not give up. When fervent prayer has prepared us, we become more than conquerors through Christ who set the example on Calvary.

47

Be sure to fear the Lord and serve him faithfully with all your heart; consider what great things he has done for you.

I Samuel 12:24

Today's disciple reads these words and wonders, "How am I to do that?" Samuel the Hebrew prophet and judge understood how it ought to be done. If the Hebrew people were to prosper, they would have to do three things—fear (hold in awe) God, serve God alone, and recall what God had done for them. In today's fast paced lifestyle that many accept as the norm, these faith disciplines are given short shrift. Even those who desire to obey the scriptural counsel are challenged by how to do it, given the real and competing demands of balancing family, career and community.

First and foremost, no matter how busy and involved you are, you must give God honor and glory when your eyes open each morning. It is a faith discipline that demonstrates you are in awe of His power and grateful for the blessing of life He provides. Many others did not share your fate. Your silent or vocal prayer of acknowledgment that it was He who allowed you to begin another day says to Him, "You alone are Lord of my life." Secondly, no matter your current station in life, you understand and accept that "It is the Lord you are serving." Whether that service is at the top, bottom or somewhere in between the ladder, you know that you are there because of God's grace, mercy and favor. So you do what you do as if you are reporting directly to Him. And finally, in everything, you utter thanksgiving and acknowledge from whence flow your blessings. Giving thanks trumps busyness every time.

48

A Creator who spoke the world into existence and then set it on a course toward eternity, supplying it with all it needed to reach that destination is a God who has a sense of adventure; in my opinion anyway. And as we've come to discover, there is certainly a sense of adventure in knowing the Lord. Think about it. When we walk with God we never know (beyond His never failing presence) what to expect or what beckons around the bend. The uncertainty of what He may have in store on any given day can raise the hair on our heads as much as daring theme park roller coaster rides. But once we accept that we serve a God who is prone to the ordinary as well as the extraordinary, we grow to appreciate and find joy in the adventures He brings into our lives. I don't think God ever intended for us to be bored or live without purpose. Just when we think we've done all we're supposed to do, we look over our shoulder and there He is; racing toward us on a loud, peace disturbing motorcycle shouting, "Jump on. There's work to be done. We need to get going!" And yet another adventure begins. Yes, we may be slow to throw that leg over and grasp Him around the waist, but once we do, we know that wherever He's taking us everything is within His control. There is joy in knowing His word is truth and will always support the thrill of the adventures we encounter with Him. Romans 8:28 says it best: *And we know that in all things God works for the good of those who love him, who have been called according to his purposes.* (Romans 8:28) Let us welcome the unexpected and often unwanted circumstances of life as nothing less than another adventure with the God in whom our faith and trust are placed.

49

I understand that we live in difficult times. Even if we wanted to pretend otherwise, the various forms of news reporting would deny us that illusion. So I suppose I should not be surprised to hear on the electronic media and read in the print format the shocking account of the fourteen year old twin sisters arrested for killing their mother. That's right; fourteen years old. According to some who knew the family, the former honor students had grown increasingly hard to handle. A few years ago they had physically attacked their mom. Following that incident they had gone to live with a great grandmother who also was unable to control them. Only recently had the mother brought the girls home in an attempt to begin anew their lives together. Those referenced in the article said they were not surprised the girls were the only suspects. Despite her efforts, the mother had continued to struggle with her wayward daughters, who appeared to do whatever they wanted.

As a believer, all kinds of questions spring to mind. Was the mother a woman of faith? Had the girls been exposed to the word of God? Was there a religious tradition within the family? Did any of them attend church? Had social agencies or anyone attempted to intervene in the earlier stages of the family's dysfunction? Rather than ponder why or how the girls could have committed matricide, the answers to the questions above might be one way to make sense of what seems a senseless act. As the justice system moves forward in the case, more information will come to light. But no matter what is revealed, followers of Jesus Christ must remember that even in such situations, God is still in control. We seek solace in His Word and understand from it that sin has consequences.

Yes, we repent of our sins and turn from wrong doing, but often the consequences remain. As disciples we are saddened by such displays of ungodliness, and when we have nothing that makes sense, we still have prayer. So we pray for these children, created by God as were we, their family and friends and for ourselves. We pray that from such great tragedy God will not only forgive but bring redemption; that this family's failures and loss will serve as springboards to wholeness for others that God will be glorified.

50

Thankfully I live in a region of the country that has a 24-7 religious music radio station. As I listen while driving the music both inspires and comforts. Just the other day as I was on my way to a meeting, an old gospel song played whose refrain is "My soul looks back and wonders how I got over." Now, I've heard that song played any number of times and this was the first time I thought, "Seasoned saints don't have to wonder how they got over; they know." Those new to their faith, testing the waters for the first time might wonder, but for those who've been on the battlefield for a while, there is no wonderment about anything that happens in our lives. After the waves of adversity and challenge have calmed and we've weathered the storm, we know without doubt from where our strength came—God and God alone. We can glance in the rearview mirror and almost see the Savior's hand stretched in our direction. Once we have accepted His call and claim upon us, we have His Word that nothing will separate us from Him and His love for us. We continue the journey, not in our own power, but by His might. *"The Lord is my rock, my fortress and my deliverer; my God is my rock, in whom I take refuge. He is my shield and the horn of my salvation, my stronghold."* (Psalm 18:2) *"The Lord is my light and my salvation; whom shall I fear? The Lord is the stronghold of my life; of whom shall I be afraid?"* (Psalm 27:1)

51

On His way to a Jewish feast in Jerusalem, Jesus passed by a pool near one of the city gates where disabled people lay, waiting for a chance to enter the pool when the water was stirred. He saw a man who had been an invalid for thirty eight years. Jesus stopped and asked the man, "Do you want to get well?"

John 5:6

Now this is where the account gets interesting. You would think anyone in the man's condition asked that question would answer without hesitation, "Yes! I do." Or in our vernacular lexicon, "Man, are you crazy? You think I like lying here like this? You (expletive) right I want to get well!" But notice the man's answer. *"Sir," the invalid replied, "I have no one to help me into the pool when the water is stirred. While I am trying to get in, someone else goes down ahead of me."* (John 5:7) He offers an excuse for his predicament rather than a direct answer to Jesus' question.

We're a lot like the invalid. In our spiritual and physical infirmities, we ignore the same question—which hasn't changed these millennia later—"Do you want to get well?" Instead we respond with excuse after excuse for why we're in our condition. Like the invalid at the pool we forget that Jesus already knows the why. He doesn't need to hear an explanation; He's asking if we have the faith to believe He can deliver us from our afflictions. The time for offering excuses is long past. Today God walks among us, in our places of dysfunction, on our beds of pain, in our closets of sorrow, in the corridors of our lives cluttered with bad decisions and arrogant choices. He strolls along, asking as He passes, "Do you want to get well? Are you tired of your condition and ready for deliverance?" The right response is "Yes, Master. Deliver me. Heal me. Restore me. Forgive me. Transform me." Let excuses fly away in the wind. Accept with joy God's response, *"Get up! Pick up your mat and walk."* (John 5:8) Let this be the day you stop excusing your situation and accept God's invitation for a life of wholeness and grace, the day when you walk in His favor.

52

A local story that filled the pages of the print media and was reported in full detail on television news reminds us that God's word is as relevant today as when it was written by our biblical ancestors. King Solomon wrote in Proverbs 3:21–22: *"My son, preserve sound judgment and discernment, do not let them out of your sight; they will be life for you, an ornament to grace your neck. Then you will go on your way in safety, and your foot will not stumble…"* Oh, had the successful young university director taken those words to heart and allowed them to govern his actions. Unfortunately, as the media reports that was not the case. And instead of anticipating the start of another promising season in his position of authority and influence, this six year athletic executive faces professional and personal disgrace and criminal charges. Why? As his stunned friends and colleagues commented, "poor judgment." Just minutes away from the beginning of a new multi-million dollar contract, the director was stopped by law enforcement officers for "erratic driving" and along with a female companion arrested for driving under the influence of alcohol.

We feel his anguish even as we wonder how he could have allowed so much to slip from his grasp. Were a few drinks and the companionship of someone other than his wife worth the risk? Biblical advice is sound. When we allow our judgment and discernment to be comprised, to lose sight of them as we go about our daily living, we risk losing the security they provide. Then instead of these faith attributes being "an ornament to grace" our neck, a provision allowing us to go our way in safety and not stumble, we experience the opposite. Scripture written over 2000 years ago is life sustaining; if we would abide by it. God's word is alive and active. It is sharper than any double-edged sword, and it judges the thoughts and attitudes of the heart (Hebrews 4:12) Just ask the athletic director whose fate hangs in the balance as I write.

53

"Anger gets in the way." That's my summation on the topic of anger management, or more pointedly, anger mismanagement. When situations arise that create discord or problems needing immediate attention, too often we respond in anger. We seek to blame. We rage at fate that has allowed the mess, disrupting the orderly routines of our lives. What we fail to realize in the heat of the moment is that the anger we feel and express does nothing to solve the problem. Quite the opposite; anger gets in the way. How? It blocks wisdom. It's impossible to respond wisely in a fit of anger.

Scripture says it even better. *"A fool gives vent to his anger, but a wise man keeps himself under control."* (Proverbs 29:11) Anger blinds us. It prevents us from settling into the stillness necessary to know God when we most need Him. Anger squashes serenity and peace. It is very difficult to center yourself so that God's spirit can offer guidance in a state of rage. Controlling anger can be a challenge when situations reel out of control; only one thing can counter it: intentionally seeking God's stillness as a first response.

To control anger we must ask God in those initial moments to give us the wisdom we need. Then we must wait quietly, in stillness for Him to respond. It may mean removing to another location, turning the proverbial other cheek, biting the tongue. Whatever it takes, if we ask and believe, God will enable us to endure the moment and give us the wisdom to handle the situation without anger ruling our response mode. Remember. Uncontrolled Anger and Wisdom will never be best buddies.

54

To paraphrase Oswald Chambers, "Faith is not intelligent understanding; faith is deliberate commitment to Jesus Christ when the way He is leading is not clearly understood." But you counter. Wait a minute. God gave us the ability to reason. He expects us to use that ability to His glory. Yes, we are blessed with the power to reason, but reasoning does not save us. Faith in God is what leads us to salvation and often that faith defies reason.

The writer of Hebrews expresses it best. *"Without faith it is impossible to please God, because anyone who comes to him must believe he exists and that he rewards those who earnestly seek him."* (Hebrews 11:6) And when we allow Jesus the lead position on our life journey, it will often require that we step out on faith and not intelligence. There's a television commercial that paints a visual of this kind of faith. The commercial is targeted to cigarette smokers seeking to break their habit. Standing atop a skyscraper, a man steps out into what appears to be thin air. He does so without hesitation as the voice over promises the product being advertised will help him lose the desire to smoke in measured steps. Then the camera swings to the unseen "steps" in the air upon which the smoker walks toward his goal of quitting. That's pretty much what our faith journey is like. Even when we don't see the path with our naked eye, we have faith that it is there; and that Jesus Himself is urging us to step out onto it. Our common sense or intelligence cautions us to "Hold up; there's nothing there." But our faith causes us to move anyway. For we understand that it is by faith that we shall be judged righteous and saved, not by how intelligent we are. Faith, not intelligence, leads us to our goal: eternity with our Lord.

Acknowledgements

In everything give thanks, for this is the will of Christ Jesus for you.

I Thessalonians 5:18 (NKJV)

And so, I do give thanks, first and foremost to my heavenly Father. It is by His grace that the seedlings of my penchant for written expression took root, and with His inspiration and prompting sprouted into reflective devotional writing.

I am grateful to family members and friends who over the years have patiently listened as I read aloud a piece I was writing or had written. Portia, Lillie, Harriette, Christa, Ridgie, Joseph, David, Trice, Donna, Bev. D, Lena, Ann, Jo, and Dianna. In so doing you have stood in the gap for Earl whose role it was to listen as each piece was finished.

"Thank you," Ann, for your critical ear whenever I called with a breathless, "Got a minute?" Without fail, you offered biblical insight that helped me refine the message. You are both my sister-friend and my "Nathan."

"Thank you," Jordan, QE, Brooklin and Logan for the joy you give your Nyanya each day. That joy uplifts and encourages me to keep up and keep going!

"Thank you," Rev. Henry L. Masters, Sr., Rev. S. Dianna Masters and Hannah's Descendants for always being here when I need you.

"Thank you," Quentin Christopher Clopton, my only son, my joy, my "Sonshine" whose personal story continues to inspire me to never stop praying, trusting, hoping, believing, and waiting on God. To God be the glory!

About the Author

The eldest of nine children, Beverly N.D. Clopton grew up in Dallas and completed her undergraduate studies in the great state of Texas before she embarked on a 40-year calling as a professional educator in the Dallas, Denver, and Los Angeles public school systems.

Stepping into retirement offered Beverly the opportunity to return to her first loves—the written word and the Word of God.

She has since published three books of devotions, including *Heaven or Bust: Journey to Glory*, *Sonshine: Reflections of Faith*, and her most recent book, *Surviving Pitfalls on the Path*.

Also Available From

WordCrafts Press

Trusting God Through Testing Times
　by Jill Grossman

Confounding the Wise
　by Dan Kulp

Pondering(s) Too
　by Wayne Berry

Ditch the Drama
　by Ginny Priz

I Wish Someone Had Told Met
　by Barbie Loflin

Youth Ministry is Easy! and 9 other lies
　by Aaron Shaver

https://wordcrafts.net

www.ingramcontent.com/pod-product-compliance
Lightning Source LLC
Chambersburg PA
CBHW030050100526
44591CB00008B/92